Gunhild Sandström

T   t
D

– H   ted
by

Chartwell-Bratt Ltd.

Printed in Sweden
Studentlitteratur
Lund 1985

ISBN/Studentlitteratur   91-44-23771-5
ISBN/Chartwell-Bratt   0-86238-095-2

TOWARDS TRANSPARENT DATA BASES
- How to Interpret and Act on Expressions Mediated by
  Computerized Information Systems

by Gunhild Sandström

Department of Information and Computer Sciences
Lund University
Sölvegatan 14 a, S-223 62 LUND, Sweden

Abstract

Computerized information systems are constructed with the
help of foundation stones based on logic for people with
varying experience. An expression mediated by such a system
could be interpreted differently by different people within
the same place of work. Also, they sometimes act or are prepared to act differently. An improved pragmatic quality of
information from computerized systems, demands expressions
explicitly extended with contexts containing the various
perspectives of the end-users. Moreover, sediment in the
organization often hinders initiatives to alter an unwanted
feature of a system. This report concerns such empirical
discoveries. It also presents some prerequisites for two
computer-based tools, which make it easier for the end-user
to interpret correctly and to use the data base more purpose-
fully. The tools make the data bases more transparent. The
posssibility for the users to initiate development of the
system, or to develop the system by themselves while using
them, is also a main message of this thesis.

Keywords

actions, augmented thesaurus, contextual descriptions, experienced knowledge, information quality, information systems,
interpretations, intervening research, keeptrack-of routine,
multi-perspective problems, pragmatics, sediment, semantics,
semantic differential, speech acts, systems development,
systems use, tacit knowledge, end-user participation

Preface

Everybody knows what information is but nobody knows the essence of it. Systems, often computerized, are constructed to fulfil people´s need of information in order to act properly. But people do not always act as if they were predictable. It happens that they behave in a rebellious fashion and do paradoxical things. More often it happens that they interpret the same piece of information differently because of different experience. These reflections were a starting point of mine when I was going to write this book.

Another starting point was the real opportunity to do the empirical research. Therefore, I am very grateful to all the people in the two organizations for their contribution to and their interest in the research. For the financial grant for the empirical work I also want to thank the Swedish Work Environment Fund and The National Swedish Board for Technical Development.

I got very valuable advice from several friends and collegues in the Department of Information and Computer Sciences at the Lund University. Especially, here I want to mention Sylvi Bille, Per Flensburg, Siv Friis and Ingrid Rehnberg for their intellectual and practical support during the last two years.

Most sincere thanks are due to Barbara Lindberg for her corrections of my English. Docent Hans-Erich Nissen deserves particular applause. He has been a wonderful supervisor and friend during this period, with our discussions hovering between fights and agreements. I have learned a lot from him, not just about information systems.

Also, I am most grateful to my husband and my children for their patience and support.

Contents

page

INTRODUCTION AND REPORT OUTLINE   1

1 EMPIRICAL WORK REALMS AND AIMS.............................6
1.1 Integration of systems development and systems use   6
1.2 Particular information systems chosen to study and to
     work with   9
1.3 Knowledge for the users   12
1.4 Users of information systems   14
1.5 The possibility of invariance-breaking   19
Summary   22
Note   22

2 BASIC PROBLEMS AND IDEAS...................................23
2.1 Pragmatic quality of information   23
2.2 Multi-perspective problems   30
2.3 Complexly related phenomena   35
2.4 Sociolects   43
2.5 Whose interpretation is the most important?   44
Summary   49
Notes   49

3 WAYS OF TACKLING ´SOFT PROBLEMS´ REGARDING INFORMATION
     SYSTEMS..50
3.1 Functions of information systems and their use   50
3.2 Views on information and its quality   54
3.3 The standardization fiat used by data base designers   56
3.4 The speech act as a new suit   59
3.5 The single-sided meaning triangle   62
3.6 The sentence ´in vacuo´   65
Summary   67
Notes   68

4 RESEARCH METHODS AND EXAMPLES OF RESULTS.................69
4.1 User and researcher participation   69
4.2 Intervening by the Sherlock Holmes´ method   70
4.3 The hermeneutic helix   73
4.4 How to generalize knowledge   74
4.5 Plans for empirical work   76
4.6 A method of inquiry   81
4.7 Measurement by Osgood´s semantic differential 84
Summary   86

5 UNDERSTANDING PHENOMENA FROM PRACTICAL LIFE..............87
5.1 Problem solving and tacit knowledge   87
5.2 Intuitive, rational and empirical knowledge   90
5.3 Sediment of history   92
5.4 Association problems   96
5.5 Strengthening and weakening words   100
5.6 The code "567" its meaning in the same information
    system   106
5.7 Opinions about computers, work and language   108
Summary   112
Note   112

6 SUGGESTED TECHNIQUES FOR PRACTICAL USE..................113
6.1 Requirements for support tools for the users   113
6.2 Decentralized team-working parts as served units 114
6.3 Some technical constructions to improve information
    systems   115
6.4 Augmented thesaurus   117
6.4.1 Multi-contextual descriptions   117
6.4.2 To update while utilizing   118
6.4.3 Outlines of multi-contextual descriptions   119
6.4.4 To represent intentional expressions   123
6.4.5 To represent perspectives behind expressions 125
6.4.6 To represent surroundings of expressions   126
6.5 Keep-track-of routine   128

6.6 Some usable programs   131
Summary   132

7 SUMMARIZING ARGUMENTS....................................133
7.1 Discoveries   133
7.2 Continuous systems development ´in the small´   134
7.3 A well-balanced decentralization of information
    resourses   135
7.4 Further research regarding the use of information
    systems   137

APPENDICES   140

A: Enkät om användning av begrepp A1-A2   140
   Questionnaires about use of expressions A3-A4   142
B: Frågeformulär och svar rörande förstärkande och försva-
   gande ord B1-B5   144
   Questionnaire and answers regarding strengthening and
   weakening words B6-B10   149
   Example of SNOMED System Information Qualifiers B11   154
C: Exempel på begrepp som ska diskuteras muntligen med
   användare C1-C4   155
   Lexikal översättning av använda medicinska begrepp
   C3-C4   157
   Example of concepts that are to be discussed orally
   with users C5-C6   159
   Lexical translation of the medical concepts used C7-C8 161
D: Undersökning av arbete, språk och datasystem D1-D10   163
   Investigation of work, language and computer system
   D11-D20   173

REFERENCES   182

Introduction and Report Outline

One of the main problems of today, within information and computer science, is to support the end-users by improving the pragmatic quality of information, i.e. the quality in use of knowledge mediated by data bases and information systems. This is what I am trying to do first by empirically investigating, whether problems from low quality of information exist and are of practical importance and next by specifying some technical tools to counter-act them.

This work concerns problems in information systems from the end-users' point of view. It will be limited to problems, which cannot, without severe distortion, be structured along only one dimension.

In different organizations, I am studying existing computer-based information systems in use, in order to make data bases more transparent in order to improve the pragmatic quality of information. The pragmatic quality is the quality that can be found in how people act or in how people are prepared to act upon mediated information.

The research is part of a program named "User Oriented Information Systems - their use and development" (Nissen et al 1982 & 1983). The aim of my work as a whole, is to develop ideas that make it possible for people to be more aware of what a computerized system can offer and how such a system can constrain. I am therefore studying differences and similarities in various people's meanings of expressions in data bases and their ensuing actions.

It is important to take advantages of the end-users' ability to take initiatives and to be creative. Organizations and individuals gain higher information quality when the end-users themselves are permitted to decide how to use and modify their supporting information system in order to do their work properly. To enable this the end-users must have fair disposal of own resources, which includes the possibilities of using computer experts at their own terms.

I intend to support the user in becoming a real co-producer of the computerized information system he/she now has to, or later, will have to employ. This differs from the user participation in systems development, which commonly takes place on the conditions of management without real end-user influence. This difference has been made clear by Kubicek (1984). A manager is, of course, an interested party in systems development, but he/she has not often the knowledge of jobs, supported by an information system in practice; and is not present when the information system is used.

A constructive part of my project is to make the users themselves modify their own systems while using them, i.e. systems development ´in the small´.

When using a computerized information system a thesaurus or a data dictionary of some kind is constructed to facilitate the search in existing data bases. It may also function as a guide to put new data into a data base. Besides these two functions, I have not seen any thesaurus which takes into account that different persons handle and use a data base differently for various reasons, based i.e. on a person´s experience, roles and intentions and on task sets. Such a tool is needed because users may attach different meanings, contents or purports to an expression stored in a data base. It may represent different phenomena to them.

Even if there is just one person developing, handling and using a personal data base, one expression in it, could stand for many different things. Yesterday when fed into the base

it had one meaning. Today it is given another and tomorrow it
may be interpreted in a third way. There may be no awareness
about the differences. In this way one person may conceive of
many phenomena but in the data base there is just one expression. This could be a problem, although only a small one. In
a multiuser system this problem becomes more obvious and more
serious. Even here we also often have just one kind of expression in the data base but which brings forth associations
with many phenomena in reality. Behind this original expression there lies probably some developer´s meaning. It represents a specific intention or experience. This may not always
be the same as that of the user. Moreover, the data feeder
and the data needer generally have different experiences and
different intentions when using a particular expression, a
data base or an information system. They also explain this
differently and they face these differences at different
times too.

Such an acquired experienced knowledge is also articulated by
Kent within the data base field (1978 p. 6) when he writes:

"A single physical unit often functions in several roles,
each of which is to be represented as a separate thing
in the information system."

They are not problems solved by traditional means. Extended
forms of homonym problems are apparent. How can we solve such
problems? Should they be solved? Are they worth solving? How
can we be sure of the meaning of expressions for specific
situations? What can be done to rouse more awareness about
these phenomena among the users? In my research these questions often appear and I have tried to find some answers. In
order to expose the fundamental nature of these problems I
will present some material from my empirical works.

The cases cover among other things how to find, test and expose the breadth and the importance of variations in meanings and interpretations of expressions in data bases. I will discuss some aspects on information in the human communication process,illustrated by the results from my studies and stressing the pragmatic and semantic aspects.

I am proposing a few new and different ways in which to go further with soft problems in order to raise the pragmatic quality of information systems. These ways are based on theories and research, which I discuss in chapters 2 and 3. In brief they involve the following, which may lead to better use of particular information systems:

* more of the combination of intuitive, rational and experienced knowledge while using and developing information systems for work related phenomena
* intentional, dynamic and contextual descriptions of concepts and sentences in more plain language and/or in more flexible structures, which should be documented in what correspond to data dictionaries of tomorrow and be made available in small pieces on the request of different users
* to form flexible messages while using information systems
* the users´ developing their information systems in the small while using them.

Systems developement ´in the small´ signifies modifications of contents and structure, made by the users themselves at almost the same time these were needed.

Work-related phenomena and work-related expressions ar two important concepts. They delimit this work to conceive phenomena in the users jobs in reality and expressions in the users language which have influence on their jobs.

I also suggest two supplementary approaches to improve user oriented information systems. I have made outlines for an ´augmented thesaurus´ and a ´keep-track-of´ routine. In this report I will present some prerequisites and presuppositions for the properties of such tools. These approaches are rather theoretical so far, but based on my experience from the participating enterprises, I am also proposing that they be applied in practice.

My report is organized with respect to what has happened in practical research work. As much of the contents is based on current empirical work, my frames and opinions have changed during the documentation. Hence the order of the contents of the report follows some of the dynamics of my research process. It is more a time axis´ contents than a strictly logical formation. However, I have tried to structure the contents as follows:
the beginning concerns realms, theories and earlier research
the middle   concerns methods and results
the end   concerns remedies and further research.

I have consciously not chosen a conventional way of presenting my work, as the changes in my frames of references and the reasons for these changes make sense only in a historical context.

1 Empirical Work Realms and Aims

1.1 Integration of systems development and systems use

There are two main activities within information and computer science, where it is urgent to make research efforts:

* to use information systems
* to develop information systems

and in both of them the users of the information systems are or should at least be involved. These two processes can be related to each other in two ways ´to develop for use´ and ´to develop while using´:

for   while

DEVELOP   USE   DEVELOP   USING

Figure 1.1: Interesting fields and their connections - realms for research

The development of an information system and the use of that system should be bound up thoroughly with each other, not only in the way that the use is a result of the development. It is also necessary to tie both the developing and the using of an information system very tightly together, i.e. to develop the system while using it. This latter connection is of great importance to me. (Figure 1.1)

Most information systems development can no longer successfully be divided strictly into a number of prescriptive or standardized phases, after a model which consists of mainly ´before´-, ´during´- and ´after´-phases in continuing top-down-analyses to bottom-up-syntheses (Sandström-Wormell 1980). An example of such a traditional model is the Systems Life Cycle model with its phases of conception, preliminary analysis, design, programming, documentation, installation, operation and cessation (Rubin 1972). More promising approaches to systems development are the adaptive design model (e.g. Keen 1980) and the prototyping model (e.g. Jenkins 1983). Such kinds of models are advocated by several practioneers (e.g. Boar 1984) and researchers (e.g Floyd 1983, Friis 1984, Sol 1983) The various moments of the phases in these kinds of approaches are more mixed, more inseparable and invisible, through a kind of learning and iterative design. These designs imply that the end users participate as users of the system on trial on a number of occasions. Hereby they will have possibilities to propose improvements and requirements to the designers of the systems before they get a new version to test. In this way they also learn about a data or information system, how it works and how to use it. A more fruitful way of evolutionary design is to let the users themselves make the trial systems and thus let them meet their own needs in a more direct way. The evolutionary design also implies that the designers of the information system learn from the potential users through their actual use and evaluation of the trial system. The users and the data experts learn from each other.

The completed information system must not be looked upon as an invariable product. Someone will act upon messages mediated by the systems or someone will act upon the system. During such use of the system, the user should either be able to make important changes or be permitted to get changes made according to his ideas and requirements. These requirements are seldom delivered at the request of a designer to the full extent in the beginning of a system´s development (cf. e.g.

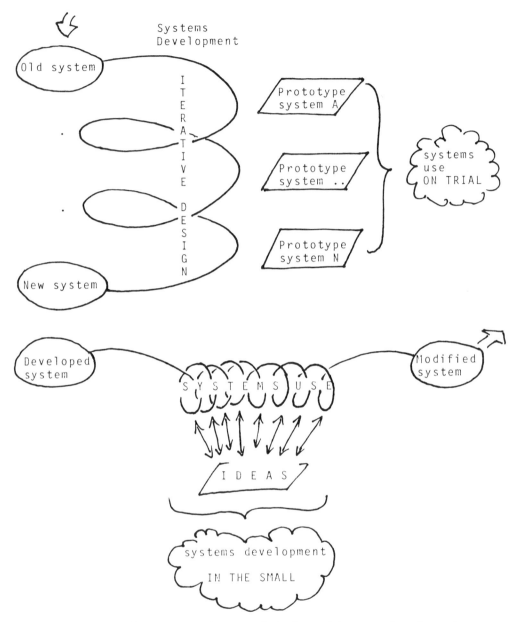

Figure 1.2: Development and use of information system bound together (Sandström 1984a)

Flensburg 1984), when the designer wishes to have them. Instead, the users will not become aware of many of these until they start to use a system. 1)

After some time the users know their system and they require more from it. Their requirements may then have risen so high or their information system may have become worn out to justify a new larger systems development. The used and modified system becomes too old. We may start a new iterative design process. (see figure 1.2)

The tight binding of the two processes together can fruitfully be divided into two types. When mainly developing, it is necessary to test and learn, and a good way of doing this is to use a prototype or a similar product, to use the system on trial. Mainly when using it, it is necessary to absorb the user's idea of improvements to the system and a good way of doing this, is to permit the user to make alterations when using the system, to develop the system in the small.

One main research goal of mine is to make it easier for the users to develop the systems in the small, while using them. I believe it is an ethical and effective way of obtaining better information systems.

1.2 Particular information systems to study and work with

I have been and I am still working with people in two big organizations, a hospital and a manufacturing company in Sweden.

The main realms, from which I show results and examples, are:
* Clinical pathology
* Clinical cythogoly   using the same particular system
* Women's clinic

```
* Export handling       using its own particular system
* Technical services    " -
```

Within these five areas I have had rather close contacts with
particular people who are doing their daily work with the
support of a particular system. This support is of various
kinds depending on these persons' different needs for their
different jobs.

In the practical applications, particular information systems
are used according to the above list. The users also utilize
other information systems, often general and overall designed
systems, but to a very limited extent. By law, some medical
reports must be made and sent to a central data file in cythological and pathological work. For central book-keeping
purposes, the administrative personnel of the Export handling
and Technical service departments furnish an overall information system with local knowledge, using information from it
once a year in order to make budgets. These are two of the
very few examples of use of systems outside their own environment.

The informations systems they are mainly using, are some
combinations of the following kinds of system characterized
by Nissen (1981 p 88):

  "A system in which a person or a group of people inform
   themselves on the topics:......, which they deem relevant
   in order to enable and/or improve their actions:......"
and
  "A system in which some people inform other (groups of)
   people on the topics:......, in order to enable and/or
   improve the actions:...... of the latter. The actions and
   the topics maybe not are chosen by the latter. These
   actions and topics may even be chosen by a third party."

The topic could be ´a person´s health´ and the users´ action could be ´to educate´ or the action might be ´to cure´. Here I am talking about an information system used by diagnosticians both to inform themselves and to inform the clinical doctors. Behind these actions and topics there are intentions, expressed and not expressed, from several groups such as politicians, doctors and clients.

Another example of a particular system is offered by the export team that handles all papers concerning import and export at the manufacturing company.

The workers inform themselves on
- available means of transport
- kinds of customer
- kinds of agents available
- different countries´ rules
- sales conditions
- payment conditions
- and so on...
in order to make correct invoices, to get profitable freight for the customers and thereby gain good-will for the company, to make alterations when the customer changes his mind, to make co-transports, etc. The users say that they cannot do this work without computer assistance and ´therefore´ there is a data system to support them.

The information system in an organization can be looked upon differently, depending on who is looking at it. A person who just acts on another person´s order may not see a system at all. They see a person, a paper or a terminal/computer, and perceive a problem. They see real things and they do not speak of systems. The decision maker may imagine an information system as something designed to support him even if he/she cannot explicitly describe it. He/she may describe a

computerized system or a data base better as they are more
concrete than the invisible information system.

For me an information system
1) is a construction for the purpose of which is to serve
people with information in an organization
2) becomes an abstraction of a service function when studied.

Taken together an information system might been seen as a
tool, a design or an object, a function, an idea or a structure. It could also be seen as a valuable possession.

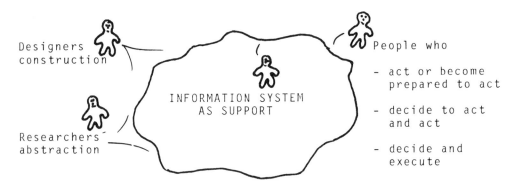

Figure 1.3: Different views on an information system

´Information system´ is a concept very difficult to define
for everybody. Those who are concerned with an information
system are either part of it or possess it, either design it
or study it. It seems abstract even though it is very concrete. I will give a more comprehensive definition through
its functions in section 3.1.

1.3 Knowledge for the users

The knowledge I acquire is rather knowledge for the consumers
of the information support, than for the suppliers of data
systems and data technology. I do not mean that the latter

group is not important or that these people could not use my results. On the contrary this knowledge may be very useful to them too. However, I am more concerned with the user side of information systems. The users/consumers may be a person, a group or an enterprise. I am mostly interested in the individual human being and the groups around a limited task or work situation.

Compared to technological research very little has been done in user oriented research concerning information systems and even less has been done for the use of such systems. But why is this field so important? Some answers from other researchers will illustrate my point:

"Computerized parts of information systems can be developed applying very simplifying assumptions about the users and their organizational settings (De Maio 1980). When a system is implemented this is always done in a real organization with real life users." (Nissen et al. 1981)

Such information systems are often designed to the designer´s ideal of a user and of an organization. This is reported by Gingras and McLean (1982) in a study measuring users´ and designers´ profiles and characteristics within the context of the design of information systems. They found that

"The designers´ "ideal user" differs significantly from the actual users´ self profile, but there was found to be no difference between this "ideal user" and the designers´ self image." (ibid. p. 169)

If this is the case it does not help the real users very much even if the designer´s purport is to be user oriented. Similar findings and reasonings about the designer, his role and his opinions of himself as a designer, have also been made by other researchers (cf. Churchman 1971; Hedberg & Mumford1979).

Even if there have been several efforts to get a more user oriented development of information systems, it is still very important to look at the use and to improve this activity and to gain experience for the development of future systems.

Moreover, the user representatives in the development processes may have been merely some kind of hostage (cf. e.g. Björn-Andersen 1976; Hedberg 1974). Also, the information need is changing and as they have learnt the system and how to use it, the requirements are extended.

For these reasons, it is very important to study the use of information systems and to acquire knowledge primarily for the end users of information systems.

1.4 Users of information systems

When diagnosing and investigating problems in information systems, it can very often be difficult to separate cause and effect. It is hard to decide whether a particular behaviour is a "people problem" or a rational response to the shortcomings of the system or other circumstances. (Alter 1980 p135)

For this reason I have done most of the empirical work together with the user when the system was used. ´My´ users I know as individuals from repeated face-to-face encounters with persons at several levels in the organisation. Before actually meeting them as individuals, I thought of the users in terms of decision makers and managers on a high level in the enterprise and of some terminal users in a scheme similar to that of Keen (Alter 1980 p 184):

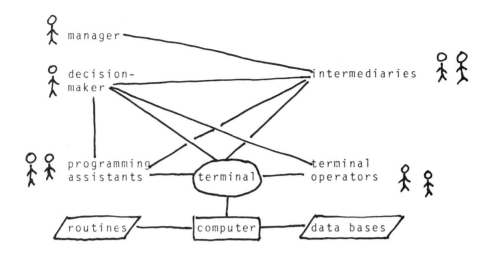

Figure 1.4: Potential users of an information system

Thus, figure 1.4 shows something of my early rough opinion about who the users might be and how they could be identified. This picture has changed as I worked together with the users themselves.

The use of an information system means to me that the information system should support the user. Knowledge of how to use the information system in order for it to become a good support system is important for the user, the designer and the researcher. This includes the fact that the properties of the information system should be wellknown to the user(s). The properties could even be improved during the use. An existing information system could thus be better used and improved through a more enriched use. The user(s) will probably also feel better.

Enterprises or society may use, much more than before, the resource ´the users´ knowledge´ supported by ´a good information system´ and then become a ´better´ organization.

Having done some empirical work, my chart of user(s) in general became a little more realistic and differentiated. The people mentioned in the figure below are concerned with information to and from the same system. The user picture was very often more complicated than I believed at first. The personal contacts were more numerous and of many more types than the arrows imply and the users can be further categorized. A number of roles and functions can be described for different working situations in an activity. (Sandström 1984a)

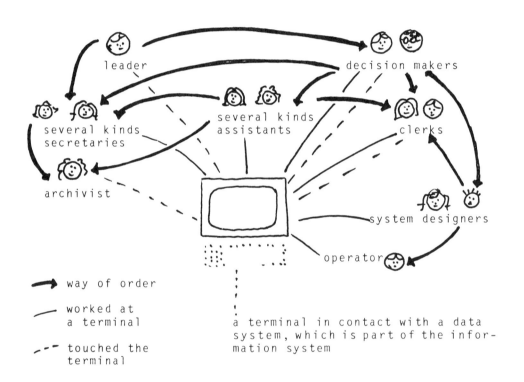

leader

decision makers

several kinds
secretaries

several kinds
assistants

clerks

archivist

system designers

operator

→ way of order

— worked at
a terminal

--- touched the
terminal

a terminal in contact with a data
system, which is part of the information system

Figure 1.5: A ´realistic´ example of users of an information
system

Figure 1.5 I made during an early stage of my work. Now the
figure seems to me a picture with many shortcomings such as

- there is no information system but just a terminal in the
  centre
- not all kinds of users are represented
- the users have not been named adequately according to their
  functions as actors in their jobs, but according to some
  function with respect to an invisible information system,
  symbolized by the terminal
- the picture is almost totally steered by Keen´s description for information retrieval (figure 1.4)

I am now redoing my example but I can tell that the description of figure 1.5 is rather true regarding people´s physical
contacts with the terminal(s).

The staff at the cythological laboratory consists of
the following 30 people:
1 archivist
1 cleaner
3 clerks, of whom 1 head clerk
17 cytological assistants, of whom 1 chief-assistant
4 doctors, of whom 1 head of the clinic
2 laboratory assistant
2 secretaries

Everybody informs themselves more or less about various objects in order to improve their own work or some related work
as a contribution to the ultimate goal "to cure sick people".
They also inform other people as they have been told to do or
as they feel is right or important to do.

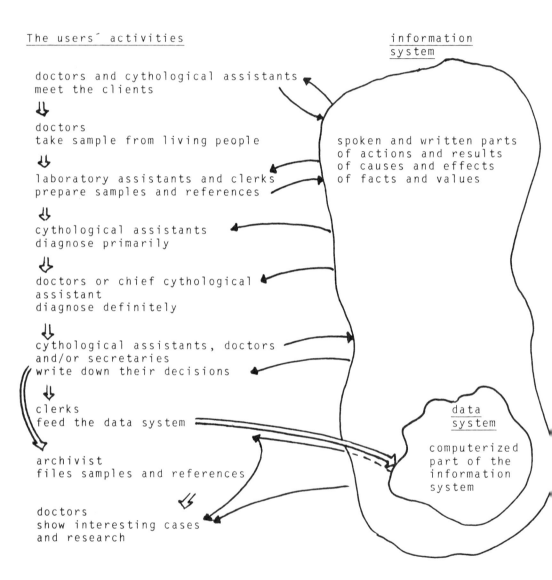

path of physical parts

information system contact

The users´ activities

information system

doctors and cythological assistants meet the clients

doctors take sample from living people

laboratory assistants and clerks prepare samples and references

cythological assistants diagnose primarily

doctors or chief cythological assistant diagnose definitely

cythological assistants, doctors and/or secretaries write down their decisions

clerks feed the data system

archivist files samples and references

doctors show interesting cases and research

spoken and written parts of actions and results of causes and effects of facts and values

data system

computerized part of the information system

Figure 1.6: Example of users of an information system from everyday life

The data system is shared by two other user groups with their own information system. The users in all three groups share both the form and the contents of the data system. The two other user groups comprise people from clinical pathology and from the women's clinic. The former group uses a data system very similar to that of the clinical cythology and the latter group uses a data system to summon people for check-ups.

I discovered that if I am ever to be able to assist the 'users' on an equal basis I had better start meeting them as professionals in their own respective professions. When describing them on paper this is very important too. Many researchers have proposed improved communication in information systems design and one way of doing this is to show genuine respect for the professionalism of the people we meet. This improves their self-esteem. In many cases that might be what is needed for them in order to effectively become co-producers of their information system.

1.5 The possibility of invariance-breaking

As I have said earlier, my area of work is the use of existing information systems. This use is a starting point of mine, in order to gather the valuable invariances which should be maintained and the interesting scientific invariances which should be broken according to the users' ideas.

In order to acquire knowledge for the users to apply as a basis for meaningful emancipatory acting in practice, I have to adopt invariance-breaking as a scientific activity. Much of this will be knowledge in order to help the users to alter habits in their way of using information systems and interacting with information systems and computer experts. This is a kind of knowledge rather different from the one usually acquired in research studies, which is knowledge in the first instance for building new technologies.

I have to look for general traces in practice. I have to look for patterns worth saving and for patterns necessary tobreak. In order to get such general traces and patterns in the social realms, I also have to do research on some kind of invariance-seeking procedure.

The two expressions invariance-seeking and invariance-breaking, I have borrowed from Galtung (1977). He says that

"A generalization is a production that is not completely singuralistic.
An invariance (law) is a generalization with a condition-set that permits variation in space, time, subject (consciousness) and object (consciousness).
A prediction is an invariance applied to future situations specified in space and time." (ibid p 73)

and further in a dialogue between an invariance seeker and an invariance breaker he - as the latter person - points out:

"I see Man and Society as more equal (than Man and Nature), they shape each other - and social science should reflect this.

...any invariance is only a stepping stone, the test of which is not whether it is confirmed by the empirical state of the world that happens to come around, but whether it shows the way to a better empirical state of the world." (ibid pp 93 and 94; the text put in brackets is my interpretation)

I propose that invariances should be accepted only as long as they serve us and then one may look for ways of breaking

them. Sometimes we enjoy invariances and sometimes we create
them. I am looking for the invariances in the form of traces
and patterns and there must be some conscious procedure of
judging the saving or breaking of the invariances. It must be
permitted for the user of an information system to break
an unwanted habit.

In a specific case someone might argue that a particular invariance is due to a law of Nature more or less in a round-
about way. Very often, however, the invariance should instead
be seen upon as a culturally/socially produced phenomenon in
jobs, and it should be broken if it constitutes an obstacle
to people willing to pay the price of breaking it.

Thus, I have to be engaged both in invariance-seeking and in
invariance-breaking scientific activities in my research. I
need to know when it is worth taking advantage of a con-
straint. In social empirical studies I look for such constraints as expressed prescriptions and restrictions or as
tacit taboos and I have found some. In one department there
were people who wrote down by hand, information extracted
from sheets produced by the data system. Well-founded or not,
they could not even think of using a terminal to extract and
process this type of work. "Never" they say. This kind of
self-inflicted restriction is hard to break. But very often
the opposite is the case, especially in group discussions. It
is rather easy, in departments where the members feel secure
in their work, to help the users to see something in a new
light. "This display lay-out might be better if we change it
in this way" or "For what do I use this, after all?" are
statements, I have encountered in my studies, which illustrate what can happen. For instance, I observed, at the end
of one of the studies, the end-users´ willingness to adopt
pictures in their information system. They have made sketches
of how to use them in forms, now used - a good step forward -
and from that it is not far away to use pictures in the com-

21

puterized part. They discussed it and they may claim equipment to make this use possible.

Summary

Great importance is attached to seeing the possibilities of developing information systems while they are being used. It is then significant to break unwanted habits. When doing this the empirical work realms are delimited to particular systems. The people I help, the end-users of the information systems, should be met as professionals in their own professions. Theoretical descriptions are often an obstacle for the researcher to see real situations, with people, jobs and problems.

Note

1) However, I do not mean that it is possible to change a system unlimitedly at any time. It is impossible to meet every requirement that can be thought of. It is not especially difficult to put constraining requirements into an information systems development or during the use of an information system. Ekenberg has reminded me (1985) of that and I will point out that I have, as he has, a more nuanced view about this matter. The requirements that appear while using information must be taken care of and handled in a fast and fair way among the users within a work team. All of them could not be satisfied to the full extent and immediately. We both realize this.

2 Basic Problems and Ideas

2.1 Pragmatic quality of information

There are two flows "from knowledge to data" and "from data
to knowledge" put together in figure 2.1, where different
levels for studying information could be separated, the pragmatic, the semantic and the syntactic levels. So far, I am
generally following Morris´ (cf. Stamper 1973) distinction in
the study of languages. However, I do not see these ´levels´
as just levels. They are rather aspects in a more tight
dependence on each other than Morris suggested.

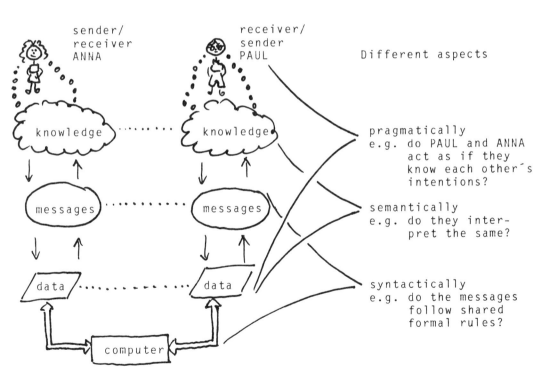

Figure 2.1: Aspects when studying information

This way of describing information aspects will serve as an illustration of where to find the part that interests me, the part of the two flows that I am studying. However, it lacks the possibility for a real multi-dimensional analysis, especially for computerized information systems, which is necessary with respect to the multi-faced meaning that can exist, at least at the pragmatic level. For the latter purpose I will use other ideas with properties focussed on the semantic and pragmatic levels.

In pragmatics, studies are focussed on the expressions and their relations to the individuals and their actions. The pragmatic aspect is about how information is used, if and for what it is used, about the intention of Anna and the opinion and action of Paul. In semantics the common meaning of the expressions used are brought into focus. The syntactic aspect focusses on data structuring and finally we also have the problem with noise in the physical transmission.

All the aspects are very important for information processing, but I am mostly interested in pragmatics and semantics when studying use of information systems and data bases. The basis for this interest I have gathered from Israel (1979 & 1982). He maintains that it is necessary to speak about real speech acts in real situations and about the logical rules in our colloquial language. The rules for the colloquial language make together a network. They could not be arranged in a hierarchical way. The base unit in analyses of these kinds is the relation, not the linguistic atom, he also says. (Israel 1982 pp 28-29) It is important to have this in focus when studying pragmatics and semantics even if it is done in a computerized environment.

I am looking for the dimensions of messages which are sent between people without or by means of a computer in the following context:

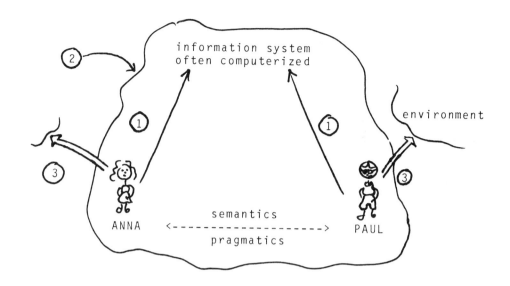

① = speech acts in real situations

② = a system of logical rules of language normally used

③ = other acts (which also can include speech acts) as
      effects of speech acts

Figure 2.2: Context for studying semantics and pragmatics 1)
           of using todays computerized information systems

ANNA and PAUL are both making speech acts in real situations
when sending messages even with the help of a computer and
they use logical rules as they know them from social everyday
life or from their normal working situations. Semantics and
pragmatics for this kind of indirect interaction between
people have to be studied a lot more.

When ANNA and PAUL can speak to each other face-to-face they
have greater possibilities to really understand the messages,
because PAUL could ask for further explanations in order to
get a correct interpretation. He could also see ANNA's ges-

tures and facial expressions. ANNA could also get an opinion of how her message has been perceived. But, if they communicate via a computer they may not get the same idea of the message. Non-verbal clues, helping to check the interpretation and the fact that the reader at least believes thathe/she has got the message, are not even transmitted. This entails a risk of misinterpretation and such misinterpretation going unnoticed. Today we may not even know who sends us a message. Even if we know the name of the sender we might never meet her/him. There are fundamental differences between different usual communication situations: ´face to face´ - ´voice to voice´ - ´letter mailing´ - ´face to display´. Different kinds of interfaces - the telephone, the paper, the television, the computer - give different kinds of constraints according to the possibilities to transmit signals. It is very important to be aware of this and inform about the constraints of the computerized system in this matter. It is also important to try to make an analysis and to make this quite clear, in order to improve existing informationsystems.

Some dimensions of a message could be:
- what a message and the very fact of sending that message now implies about the relation between ANNA and PAUL. This in itself may call for several dimensions/levels, e.g. what ANNA feels about PAUL, what ANNA believes PAUL feels about her, etc.
- intentions of ANNA, her apprehension of and her belief in PAUL´s intentions (in the situation) etc.
- some facts contained in the message.

In principal one could set up a table, consisting of different parts of the environment, of the messages exchanged from the viewpoint of human beings as users - receivers and senders - of that information.

	affections	meanings	actions & their	results
.	...	...	...	...
.				
.				
ANNA´s	feelings	significations	working	products
	intentions	connotations	problem solving	problems
	opinions	expressions	decision making	solutions
	purports	indications	execution	knowledge
	...	...	...	...
PAUL´s	feelings	...	...	...
.	...	...	...	...
.				
.	and so on...			

Figure 2.3: Different contexts when interpreting information

ANNA´s and PAUL´s feelings, intentions, opinions and so on
could fit in or not, in various combinations. This depends
naturally on their different experiences and possibilities,
what they know and what they can do. An information expert
must find out what is important for those who are to use the
systems and take that into account in his/her model if he/she
is building a system from a model. The alternative, in a more
process-oriented approach, is to build into the method a
consideration for this in the developing process and in the
continuing use.

The relations of linguistic expressions to people and their
actions as an interactional phenomenon are not always direct
between people and therefore not quite clear. We might have a
computer between the people, who are meant to interact. We
then have a time and space distance between them. The computer may in itself become an impacting factor. Perhaps we
should talk about a broken relationship in such a case. To
modulate these thoughts of extremes I would rather say that
there is surely a difference between ´face-to-face informing´
and ´informing with the help of computers´. The semantical
bandwidth of a computer as a channel in man-to-man communication is - and will for a long time remain - smaller than in a
face-to-face situation. (Nissen 1976) However with free text

comments, pictures, video etc. the computerized information system can become much broader than it is in traditional systems.

If syntactics is the study of data and their relations to other data, we can say that semantics is the study of expressions and their relation to the ´outside world´. The question is ´what is the meaning of a certain expression?´

Semantics, when used by logicians, refers however to theory expressed in meta-language, abstracted from all use, and concerns rules relating to expressions and meanings. Semantics is then on an artificial level and treats language as a calculus. Words and sentences are constructed by the logician, who works with a formal language. It represents an abstraction from real life situations.

We can also look upon semantics from analytic and substantial arguments. Statements, for which one only needs to look to the formal language and its rules to decide, if they are correct, are called formally valid. They are used in analytic argumentation, in which verifying backings of warrants ipso facto means veryfing conclusions. Against this kind of reasoning stands substantive argumentation, for which correspondence with phenomena outside the formal language has to be checked. (Toulmin 1958, pp. 123-127, 132)

But semantics in linguistics is also a term employed by others to denote ´theories of meaning´ from users in a specific environment. I adhere to such a view of semantics because it is more closely related to the study of communication. (cf. Cherry 1957)

To me ´to know´ and ´to inform´ belong to quite different spheres. For instance ´to want´, ´to know´ and ´to feel´ belong to one kind of concept but ´to inform´ belongs to a

second and ˙to divide into data˙ or ˙put together from data˙
belong to a third group of concepts:

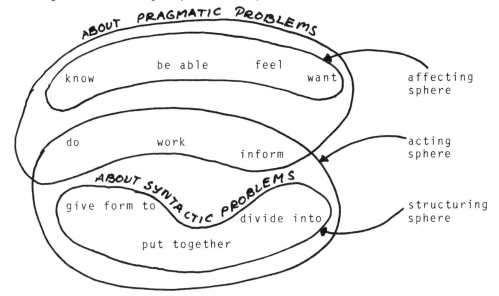

Figure 2.4: Different pragmatic spheres of result because of
          differently perceived information

I want to distinguish between ˙informing˙ a person and ˙gi-
ving form to˙ knowledge. According to the way I see it,
˙informing˙ could lead to pragmatic problems but ˙giving form
to˙ is a structural concept, even if both of them belong to
an acting sphere.

All the verbs in the above figure belong to pragmatics even
those which are about syntactical problems in a structural
sphere. Something is happening and we feel or do something
about it. My example is limited to patterns relevant for
working situations and it is not complete. I mean that such
an overall perspective is important when building and using
information systems.

This way of not completely separating the syntactive level of
a language from other levels, I have also found in Winograd

(1973). There he shows, within the field of programming, how
a general view of language can be filled in with enough
material to provide a working model for question-answering
systems. He proposes that such systems have to deal with the
entire language process. He has written programs with emphasis on the interaction between three domains, manifested by
"a syntactic parser which works with a large-scale grammar of
English", by "a collection of semantic routines that embody
the kind of knowledge needed to interpret the meanings of
words and structures" and by "a cognitive deductive system
for exploring the consequenses of facts, making plans to
carry out commands and finding the answers to questions"
(ibid. p. 154).

2.2 Multi-perspective problems

Part of my research goals could also be seen as a research
problem extending to the decision support field, where the
research mainly concerns situations that are not quite structurable (Gorry & Scott Morton 1971). In my work, however, I
also prefer to concern myself with what I propose to be
called, multiperspective situations or problems. We then have
three groups of problems to be concerned with:

* well-structured problems
* ill-structured problems
* multiperspective structurable and restructurable
  problems

The last group is parts of the other two groups. Muiti-per-
spective problems implies new kinds of requirements from
support in decision making.

A main kernel of the research idea is to find and present
problems of the second or third kinds from real working

situations. These problems are not easy to solve or may not
be solved at all by formal logic of today. These are intuitive problems and as such they are often known as experienced
problems.

"Real world problems are what have been termed ill-structured. ... Ill-structured problems are problems for which
the definition of the problem is not clear or ´given´
beforehand." (Mitroff 1980 p. 187-188)

The non-givenness of real world problems is extensively discussed by Checkland (1981). He defines a real world problem
to be

"A problem which arises in the everyday world of events and
ideas, and may be perceived differently by different people.
Such problems are not constructed by the investigator as
are **laboratory problems.**" (ibid. p. 316)

and a soft or unstructured problem to be

"A problem, usually a **real-world problem**, which cannot be
formulated as a search for an efficient means of achieving
a defined end; a problem in which **ends, goals**, purposes are
themselves problematic." (ibid. p. 316)

The multiperspective structurable problems are problems
that in order to be properly treated, need to be seen from
several independent perspectives. These pers ectives might
depend on different human roles and different tasks in a
piece of work. The reason for presenting and/or analyzing
them as more than one-dimensional ones, is also the different experience of the people involved and their different
intentions. Thus, the independent dimensions are
- ´users´ different intentions´
- ´users´ different experience and knowledge´

- ´different languages of user groups´
- ´time when the expression was sent or received´
- ´time when the message is valid´
- ´the environment of the expression emanating from the actual task within the job´.

By independent, I do not mean independent to 100 %, but independent enough, not to permit a simple transformation into one dimension in an ortogonal system.

I am not looking for problems which are more-dimensional in physical space such as e.g. for calculating trajectories of rockets in order to control space flight. I am rather looking for soft problems with the intentional, contextual and changeable features.

Nissen and Checkland have spoken about ´problematic situations´. Nissen (1981) conceives them as inherently ill-structured problems. Checkland (1981) conceives them as interplays of real world events and ideas which at least one person perceives as problematic and worth investigating.

Such problematic situations could sometimes be handled in a computerized environment in such a way that new opportunities to exploit and new chances to take can be missed. An example is the standardized way to date a fact in a computerized system. I have found a possibility to counter-act these tendencies, when speaking about problems as not being one-dimensional. There could be problems with characteristics to be structurable, then structured and thus more visible. The problematic situation contains ill-structured problems, some of which may be clarified by structuring according to some recognizable dimensions, for example ´users´ intentions behind´, ´times when defining´ and ´surroundings of a expression or a sign´.

´Problematic situations´ are often represented in information systems, in sentences and words or in messages and data, but in a rather fragmentary way. The point is that they might be better anchored to meanings, history and context. A view of this kind is documented by Checkland (1981) through advocating the ´rich picture´ of the ´problematic situations´ before extracting something for problem solving. The rich pictures are used during systems development of more overall character before defining and analysing (Checkland 1981, Wilson 1984). However, I imagine that such pictures could be very useful also when carrying out systems development ´in the small´. For my purposes now, I just want to talk about ´problematic situations´ no matter how they will be described.

The problems from a problematic situation, most likely described as above, and concerning me, can be illustrated as in figure 2.5 below. Both ´problematic situations´ and the rest of the figure 2.5, might belong to the real world for the users as problem solvers and also for them as systems designers. These two functions should become real to them, even if the analyzing and designing parts might be done by more abstract thinking and modelling. I am implicitly speaking of the fact that the users may analyze and redesign the information system in order to avoid time lag. This supports my idea of systems development ´in the small´.

The word "structurable" stands for ´intentionally structurable´, ´contextually structurable´ etc. Any kind of problem within limited working situations has to be looked at from the beginning as ill-structured as I do not know until later on whether the problems are structurable or not. Also, I do not know if they might be better described by a contextual environment or a dynamic explanation, by history and intention, for instance. They could also be classified as ill-structured, because of their many dimensions that cannot

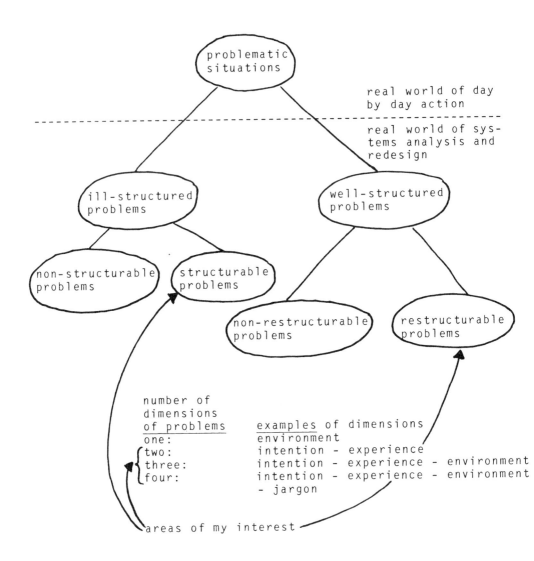

Figure 2.5: Problem areas 2)

easily be seen. I cannot, for the moment, take into account
many dimensions, just three or maybe four so far. A well-

structured problem might be well structured according to some other parameters that the users have in mind and might be able to restructure according to their intentions.

In this thesis I do not deal much with non-structurable, ill-structured problems or well-structured problems not restructurable or with problems of just one dimension. The latter may just exist as a human artifact easy to handle and manipulate. It may, however, not exist as real world problems, such as ´whose words will be the right ones without having any indication of the problem at all, not even unconsciously´.

2.3 Complexly related phenomena

In systems development the terms and the sentences/messages that are to be stored and used later on, are elucidated with respect to their meanings in ways the systems experts, the computer suppliers and the programmers make visible in structures around the data contents, which are to be available in the future. They generally store:
- schemas of expressions and their relations (one or several kinds of data base schemas)
- elementary and/or compound message types, where the expressions from the schemas, and only these, are used.

Usually the whole messages are not stored in the way they normally appear in print or utterances. First their propositional forms are stored, and then the values of the variables are put into the data system. Thus: first the schema and the propositional forms and then the data, i.e. the variable contents of propositions mediated.

The schema in a sense becomes the only, limited and closed, context of interpretation of messages mediated by a data processing system. A human interpreter in ordinary conversa-

tion, if needed, brings in wider contexts, if e.g. an interpretation within a narrow context does not make good sense to
him. In cases where he receives messages through a data
system, he is today not able to do this.

In connection with the data input process regarding important
expressions, their meanings are implicitly interpreted by the
data feeder or by the person who ordered the input process to
take place. In this case the leader in the figure 2.6 below
can be a person with an intention of choosing the expression
that shall be put into the system. The intention is manifest
by the very choice of a particular expression. It may be
reconstructed by others from this choice in its context. But
the intention is not to be found in the expression as such.
The expression is exactly the same as if used by someone else
with a different intention in another context.

The development and the input may have occurred yesterday,
last week, a year ago, that is AT THAT TIME, which gave one
meaning. The retrieval of expressions is going on NOW, which
may give another meaning. Even if the person who develops,
feeds or retrieves, is one and the same human being, the
signification need not be the same from time to time. The
human being alters his opinion, his environment, he has new
experiences and thereby the meanings of the expressions used
will change as well. Of course this is also the case when
talking about the time perspective, AT THAT TIME - NOW -
LATER ON. In the process of retrieval there may also be
several people involved and an expression might for this
reason get still more meanings.

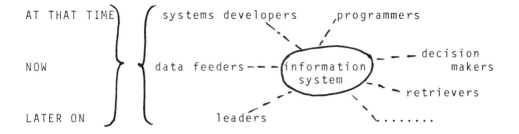

Figure 2.6: People that may have or may give meanings to
expressions in information systems at different
times

This actually means that different interpreters may assign
various meanings to one and the same expression. Short expressions are used when we want to communicate about phenomena, which could be physical events, ideas or experienced
phenomena. People conceive meanings for the words they use in
contexts depending on their intention or experience, or they
could even depend on statistical prediction. I am sure it is
possible to find several more perspectives and also other
ways of classifying them. Expressions have or will get different meanings due to all these factors and also due to
alterations over the time.

A structure composed of these ideas, according to figure 2.7,
might be a contribution to information systems theory. By
this I mean that the structure could serve as an advisory
element in the systems design and redesign. The advice is to
users/designers, to find out about different kinds of perspectives, phenomena, experiences and times in order to express meanings and make it possible to gather these meanings
from the expressions referred to, when the system is used.

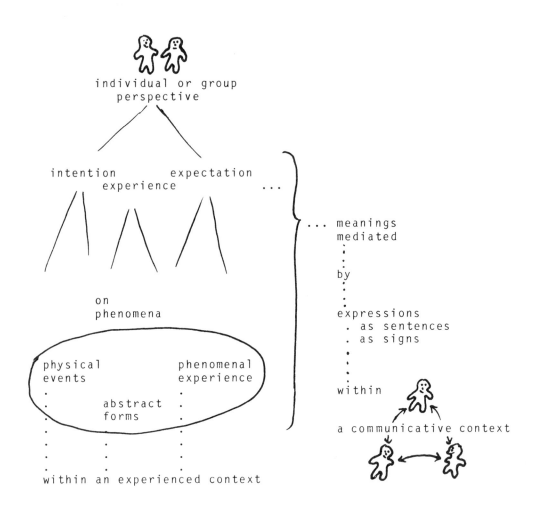

individual or group
perspective

intention   expectation
    experience   ...

on
phenomena

physical   phenomenal
events   experience
.   .
    abstract   .
    forms   .
.   .   .
.   .   .
.   .   .
within an experienced context

... meanings
mediated
.
by
.
expressions
. as sentences
. as signs
.
within

a communicative context

>-->time

Figure 2.7: Phenomena, expressions and meanings in view of
            contexts and time

To achieve some parts of the figure, I got very good support from Bergmann (1964) regarding the triad of phenomena and from Watzlawick et al.(1967) and Lindholm (1979) regarding the meaning of expressions.

Meaning evolves, in interplay between a phenomenon, an individual and a culture. It is important to recognize the dependence of meaning on history. A person will assign meaning to a phenomenon depending on the history of the culture he is a part of, what society and what group he belongs to as well as on his biography. (cf. Lindholm 1979)

In order to check the validity of an idea we have about a phenomenon, we have to communicate with others. In order to communicate an idea we have to find some expression for it. We have to frame what is to be said against a background (cf Bateson 1972) but such a frame must, at the same time, not be too constraining. The frame must be changeable and must contain enough context or refer to its context in some way.

A phenomenon can be explained in relation to the structures of which it constitutes a part and from the structures it includes. An expression can evoke different kinds of wholes in the reader/hearer. It can also be described as part of a working situation.

As Wedberg (1945 pp. 10-12) has pointed out, important phenomena in the social sciences often seem to be interconnected by n-ary relations (n>2). In order to explicate social phenomena one often needs to present several phenomena simultaneously and indicate how they are related. To communicate our explications we are again forced to employ expressions.

Without claiming completeness, I am pointing out some kinds of possible contextual milieu for an expression in order to clarify its meaning:

´to complete with a relation´ for instance a phenomenon
has given an effect in terms of actions
and reactions and we need to describe this

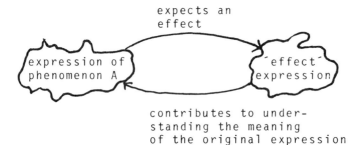

expects an
effect

contributes to under-
standing the meaning
of the original expression

´to complete with surroundings´ for instance a phenomenon
must be extended with its impacting area

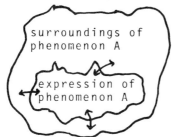

´to complete with hidden translations´ for instance an
expression can be understood more clearly
with other words or another language or
within another paradigm

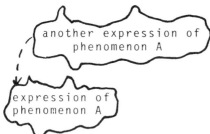

Figure 2.8: Some complementary contexts clarifying an
expression

Outside a contextual frame, an expression or an idea might not be understood or totally misunderstood. In many cases these contexts are very natural. In daily work it is probably very often so. The contexts are present implicitly. Still this cannot always be expected to be the case. When it is not, "a phenomenon remains unexplainable as long as the range of observation is not wide enough to include the context in which the phenomenon occurs." (Watzlawick et al.1967 pp.19-21)

My conjecture is that it is very important to find out when and where ˊthe observation is not wide enoughˊ to really explain a phenomenon, especially in cases where the communication takes place by means of a computer.

The ˊeffectˊ expression above could be supplemented with a ˊcauseˊ expression and there is a historical chain, a kind of time dimension. When the meaning of an expression varies between individuals, maybe with different contexts, we have a spatial dimension. There can be awareness or not of different opinions. This is a third component. If the opinions are about a human being, the awareness of this human being is a factor too. (cf. Galtung 1977, Lindholm 1979)

The emphasis is on the larger contexts which have been abandoned, lost or not yet found for some reason. Jargon and opinions, causes and effects, history and intentions can be needed to complete expressions in order to improve the pragmatic quality of information systems use.

Another problem is that it is very difficult to get objective meanings for expressions in data bases. By this I mean that it is hard to get inter-subjectively shared interpretations of expressions mediated by data bases, simply by standardizing their names and formal relations to other standardized expressions in the same data bases. It seems impossible, if only the lines of attack attempted so far are followed. Now there are hopes of permitting multi-perspective expression through explications of context of natural language and through representation with the help of new logics (cf Haack 1978 & Nilsson 1984).

The users must decide how this will be carried out when using computers and see to it that they are aware of what has been decided and that they have the opportunity to re-decide. It is sometimes necessary to re-decide both for their own sake and the effectiveness of the whole organization. And - a meaning of an expression may probably not last for ever, because the world is not yet complete.

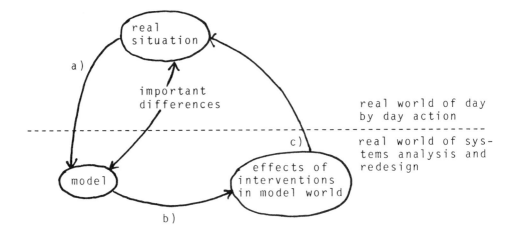

a) abstract modelling
b) manipulation by experiment on model
c) model interpretation in order to undertake an intervention
   in the problematic real situation

Figure 2.9: Important differences between real situations
            and models 3)

When describing the contextual milieu of ideas or expressions for analyzing or transmitting purposes, this is done by using some kind of model. At the best, this work is done with homomorphic models, which have to show essential features corresponding to the system modelled (cf. Beer 1966). As models are simpler than reality, it is a matter of using applied symbolism to diminish the distance to reality, maybe by using some kind of ´rich pictures´ or ´popular graphs´ in early stages (cf Checkland 1981; Nissen & Andersen 1977). To point out the important differences that are to be diminished, I will use the figure 2.9 above.

How far these differences are diminished, is a question of practical consideration in each case. What is important is to remain aware of the differences, particularly when interpreting the model, in c) in the figure 2.9, as this interpretation is often undertaken by a different group of people, from the one which undertakes the modelling and experimenting parts. The differences are not ´epsilons´ to be presupposed as almost negligible. They must definitely be taken into account, both qualitatively and quantatively, when developing and using information systems on both a large and small scale. The direct involvement of the end-users when analyzing and redesigning an information system and the awareness of real constraints in a system, or of differences between models and real situations, contributes to the possibilities to make good decisions and actions. The pragmatic quality may thus be raised within the work in question.

2.4 Sociolects

Previously I have spoken of jargon and jargon language in enterprises and I am anxious to introduce sociolects that exist in or around a task or a place of work.

Wunderlich talks about language-families (1979 pp 331-347) and distinguishes between different degrees of abstraction:

* linguistic system of an individiual person
* homogeneous linguistic system for a group, relative to particular situations of use
* dialectal and diatypic characteristic varieties of a language at a given time
* individual language at a given time

With this rather rough but useful classification, I will look for sociolects of relatively similar linguistic activities used by groups of people with the same task or in similar working situations, i.e. the second linguistic system above. These sociolects are important in daily work when using information systems, where not every individual can have his own personal system to use. They are part of, or the same as, the working jargon language.

An investigation of the language used, the work jargon language, will serve the purpose to compare the language actually used, with the presupposed one in the data base schemas. Maybe there is a need for modification in the data base.

It is important for the quality of an information system to gather this kind of information, maybe as a by-product, when developing it or studying its use. There should be great use for such by-products in the tools, which will be described in the chapter on "Suggested techiques for practical use".

2.5 Whose interpretation is the most important?

This question implies a choice which is not at all trivial. But even if there are many wills in a work team, this must not be taken as a reason by a designer to decide once and for all how to form messages in information systems.

The most usual meaning of an expression is often equal to a ´normal´ meaning, or to an ´objective´ meaning of the expression. Such an expression can also be said to be objectivized by this usual meaning. A similar reasoning is made by Barthes (1964) concerning pictures. He thinks that in an aesthetical perspective a denotated message can appear as a kind of original state of a picture. A picture, theoretically made free from its connoting values, could be seen as fully objective. I mean, like Barthes, that such pictures do not exist, and I also mean that fully objective written messages are very few in reality. But we may need to point out the most common meaning, attached by:

* an individual
* a working team
* a department or
* an organization.

The most common meaning in a group must be agreed upon within its members. The end-users themselves have to decide. However, a great danger is that the meaning will be "canned" (Lindholm 1982) and ´sterilized´ and that an ´expert language´ and a ´group jargon´ will be fortified when having a main meaning.

In order to illustrate the difference between the common meaning of an expression and some other meanings I will use an example from my clinical cythology study. If we look at the expression ´biopsy´ the most common meaning, within the department, is ´to look at living materia´. A number of other meanings exist in the rest of the definitions (see chapter 5.4). In another working situation or on another occasion, a connoting property can very well be denoting. A driver´s license denotes usually the right for a person to drive certain types of motor vehicles. On another occasion, for example before the bank counter, the driver´s license may be used as an identification card and then denotes that ´you are

45

you´. This concerns the choosing of parts of information contents to represent total knowledge.

By introducing possibilities for the end-users to create their own structures for written messages, there will be a more flexible milieu for correctly interpreting a message mediated by a computer, what it connotes and what it does not connote. The user should be able to use several kinds of structures to represent the contents of a message. It must also be permitted to show explicitly the connotations of an individual through a structure or a sign. Here I mean that it is important to recognize the fact that to human interpreters one or a few symbols often stand out as a ´gestalt´ for a whole. This is not necessarily a 🚶 . It might as well be a 🧍 . Both could stand for a man. The same reasoning could be used for the ´message´ introduced by Langefors (1966) and a sentence in another structure, both representing the same contents. It must be possible to choose the structure in which to form knowledge. This structure then becomes a part of a whole, a part that gives some important features which might show for instance the intentions of the sender of the message. Information can in this sense ´be intentional´, be purposeful. (cf. Nurminen 1980)

Similar to this way of thinking, is the representation of ´pars pro toto´ according to Watzlawick (1978). It concerns analogic relations between signs (pars) and the whole (toto) that they signify. A ´pars pro toto´ representation exists when a certain part stands or is interpreted to stand for a whole and when this grasping of reality is a global holistic perception of totalities. The totality may contain complex relationships, patterns, configurations and structures, but just one little property is needed to recognize this totality. This one property that represents the totality could be recognized by a group of users or could be recognized by an individual.

If you associate to "the Italian cooking" by means of "the colours of the Italian flag on canned food", here a connoting message of an advertising effort (that denotes "buy this food") is ´the pars´ for the Italian cooking which is ´the toto´. The signifying and the contextual differences here are very difficult to see or to imagine, and I do not know yet if this matters. However, in this example, the advertising purpose of information is evident.

An impression that a person gets of a situation or of several situations in an ordered or accidental way, might serve as a model for a message structure. This is rather close to associative thinking but this reflecting and creating procedure is more strict and formal and conscious, even if experienced knowledge is used in the shaping. When associating, a person also uses this kind of knowledge, but more freely and more unconsciously. In this latter case a man does not think of any systems or any constraints.

To shape such a structure means to see patterns of information/data/phenomena in situations similar to each other. The ´message´ defined by Langefors (1966) is just one result of this forming. I introduce this in order not to let a certain structure be outstanding, ´controlling´ much of the information system.

The new thing about this is the user´s possibility and way of making structures herself/himself, i.e. that each message could be formed at any time and we do not always know its structure in advance. We must offer more flexible systems that may handle these types of difficulties.

Boland(1978) has found, that equality have influenced the result positively in systems development. Boland showed that higher quality designs with important implementation advant-

ages were produced, if there was an initial sharing of information and mutual suggestions, followed by a critique of each
other´s suggestions in the interactive process between experienced systems analysts and nurses.

I assume that more equal relations between users and designers also might influence the use of an information system. It
might be done by using the possibility to create message
structures more freely while using the information system.
Preceded by shared information by the system users, the message structures might even be a sociolectal result within the
users´ jargon environment.

A problem arises when sharing a data base outside a group or
a team of persons, who know the convention of their information system. By letting other persons in, the data base will
be used by people who do not share an opinion on which conno-
tations/properties distinguish the entities reported on via
the data base. The decision taken on which one to choose for
each particular entity or relationship amounts to deciding
"whose interpretation is most important".

In order to identify differences in what various expressions
connote to different users, it is important for the users
and me to gather the different opinions of their work. I let
users answer questions both freely and in a questionnaire, in
order to get such opinions. The answers will serve as feed-
back to the users themselves and as background for me when
interpreting phenomena.

Unambiguous denotation has so far dominated the scene and
connotations of entities have been their properties. These
are seen as homogeneous throughout every particular set of
entities or entity type. To allow these connotations, properties to be open to change, by users during use and over
sets of entities, seems both a challenge to data base theory

48

of today and a possible decisive step forward for data base praxis of tomorrow.

A good alternative, after all, might be a more frequent use of ´natural´ language in texts in information systems, as we share the rules for the natural language to a greater extent than those for a computer-based one. We have, in general, grown up with the rules for our mother tongue.

Summary

The fundamental problem which I find concerns the end-users very much, is the question of how the pragmatic quality of an information system can be improved. When measuring improvements of ´pragmatic quality´, it is the users´ actions or the possibilities of actions that have to be evaluated. Such evaluation has to be undertaken by the users themselves. Improved quality, claims for expressions explicitly extended by the users´ several perspectives. Such requests are expressed in terms of contextual, people-related and time-related descriptions. The quality concerns also the question of how an interpretation of an expression, shared by a group, can be improved.

Notes

1) The basic reasoning for the structure in this figure was performed together with Professor Joachim Israel in February 1985.

2) The fundamental idea of dividing the figure 2.5 into the two ´world´ parts, emanates partly from Checkland (1981 p. 163 figure 6).

3) The figure of the "Important differences between real situations and models" was suggested by Nissen in November 1984.

3 Ways of Tackling 'Soft Problems' Regarding Information Systems

3.1 Functions of information systems and their use

Within any organization there is always some kind of information system. Traditionally such a system has been perceived as comprising sub-systems for collecting, processing, storing, and distributing information (Langefors 1966). These subsystems became apparent when we started to design computerized information systems.

It is not enough that systems mediate information, which can be made available through a distribution phase. It must also be possible to decide oneself what we actually want from the systems. This may be decided in advance once and for all by users and expressed in requirement specifications. To a great extent, however, this is not enough. In spite of the fact that requirement specifications must be redone several times or that we use an adaptive design, requirements turn up which need to be met by a retrieval phase. Such a phase becomes then an alternative and a supplement to a predictable distribution of information.

There still exist traces from large batch processing as the only alternative in early computer use. Only at the price of a huge surplus capacity, could we offer short turn around time of small jobs to meet the user´s demand with access only to batch processing.

For these reasons I propose a broader definition of information systems which includes the one given above.

A)

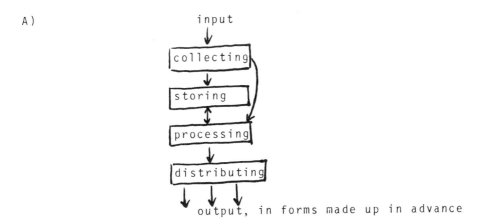

Figur 3.1 A: Yesterday´s functions of information systems in organizations

B)

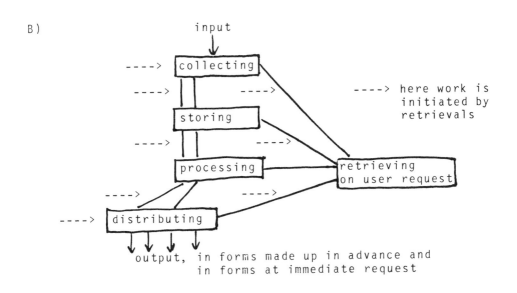

Figure 3.1 B: Today´s functions of information systems in organizations

Demands for information retrieval, initiate and create work
in other parts - actions and interactions - of an information
system. An informtion system becomes more dynamic and adaptive, when it includes a retrieval function. In fact this
phase has been in practice for several years in many information systems in use, but it has not been suggested in theory
as a main integral part of the system, and with evident
effects upon other parts.

In one of the organization I have studied, every system but
one has a retrieval function, which facilitates work according
to the end-users. But in my opinion, they seem remarkably simple and they are not as flexible as I imagined. They were based
on very simple display menus and there were very few possibilities of choice. More awareness of the potentialities in
retrieval capabilities of information systems might be useful.

When talking about support from information systems, there is
an underlying statement that the system is serving someone
and I am then thinking of the end users in an enterprise, in
a group or team and as individuals. I see information systems
as tools to support and facilitate work and look upon their
use as an active retrieval and an active work operation,
where the users
 * learn
 * are engaged
 * take responsibility
 * create
 * initiate
to a great extent. In short, the users - as exemplified in
section 1.4 - might function better and might also do better
work. But this presupposes that management looks upon all
workers in an organization in this way, i.e. as McGregor
(1960) theory Y people. Even if management is doing so, some
of the workers look upon themselves as if management does not
see them as especially independent.

Computer people first identified the demand for sometimes
one and sometimes another piece of information of their own
choice, among managers. As a counteraction, decision support
systems then became of a different character than the older
electronic data processing.

Alter (1980 p. 1-3) points out some main distinctions between
decision support systems (DSS) and most electronic data processing (EDP) systems roughly as follows:

DSS focus on	EDP focusses on
- active use	- passive use
- line, staff and management activities	- clerical activities
- overall effectiveness	- mechanical efficiency
- the present and the future	- the past
- flexibility and ad hoc utilization	- consistency and trans- action processing

The use of the DSS is intended to increase the effectiveness
of individuals in several ways, or rather, expressed asseve-
ral kinds of results that show
- improved personal efficiency
- better expedited problem solving
- facilitated inter-personnel communication
- promoted learning and training
- increased organizational control.
This has been empirically found according to Alter (ibid. pp.
95-104).

In particular the fact must be stressed that the initiatives
come from the user of the system and the emphasis on flexibility and non mandatory utilization. These basic factors be
long according to my opinion to all good information systems,
their design and use. The effects which have been found by
Alter assure me that I am going along the right lines.

3.2 Views on information and its quality

´Information´ is a word very commonly used. It stands in my opinon for anything between wisdom and ´data´. It is used both colloquially and scientifically and in the latter case differently within different sciences.

The concept ´wisdom´ will not be used in this report, but it is necessary to explain that its classical meaning covering both ´values and knowledge´ is here taken over by the concept ´knowledge´. Thus, ´knowledge´ is used to cover both facts (´knowledge´ in olden times) and values. (cf. Siu 1957)

An information system is only justified, if it is possible to gain ´knowledge´ from it or by means of it. However, ´information´ is not equivalent to ´knowledge´ according to my way of thinking. ´Information´ emanates from the Latin word ´informare´ and means ´to give form to´. I mean we give form to ´knowledge´. We formalize ´knowledge´. Lindholm expresses this as "canned knowledge" (1982 p. 3).

Langefors discusses information in terms of ´messages´ and he states a minimal structure needed to enable someone to inform by means of a message outside the ´here and now situation´ informed about, i.e. with some presuppositions as to the limits of context. The conditions that must exist explicitly or implicitly, so that we can formalize, are the following: You need to know what system you are talking about, what object in the system you observe, what you observe about the object and when this observation is relevant. This is the general structure of a ´message´ according to Langefors (1966). If there is just one property to measure, this ´message´ is called an ´elementary message´ (ibid.).

A ´message´ can be meant to give ´new knowledge´, but for a
receiver of the ´message´ the ´information´ could be new, be
already known or be pure rubbish. In these cases we are
dealing with human processes of interpreting messages, i.e.
some symbols/signs or structures constructed in order to
mediate knowledge.

´Messages´ can consist of ´signs´, letters or phonemes. It
can also be said that ´data´ are parts of ´messages´. ´Data´
according to Langefors (1966) do not give any ´information´.
For example: RED, R, E and D are meaningless whithout any
semiotic context (´The carpet is RED´). In the context of
data bases, however, "data" often stand for facts, i.e. ´mes-
sages´ or ´elementary messages´, one of which contains an
identification, variable type, variable value and time. (cf.
Teorey & Fry 1982)

Ivanov extended the elementary message with a term containing
accuracy and precision of the measuring process. This was a
step forward to a quality awareness, much needed in information use. At that time he also showed the necessity of explicitly stating the relation of the message to the system/envi-
ronment. (Ivanov 1972) Before that the system/environment was
looked upon as something which everybody knew. Therefore it
was almost never explicitly written down in the messages.
This is also the case in many working situations today. The
environment is taken for what it is.

The surroundings of an identification were implied by Langefors (1966) in a ´full´ message but this was not developed
more than there was, in the message, a system in which we
found our point to measure. He also speaks of the receiving
structure, where the received data are to be interpreted.

To imply contexts is not enough. The historical and intentional contexts are needed to be explicitly expressed in

order to improve intersubjective sharing of interpretations. The context of the sender, of the sender's message, as well as of the receiver is necessary. There will definitely be no adequate action without them and it is the action that counts. The value of a message (mediated by a computer) finally depends upon how its receiver acts or changes his/her preparedness for action. This could be called its instrumental value. For the message-receiving actor there is a value in acting ethically right. This could be called the intrinsic value of the action to the actor. As long as the actor perceives his/her action to be ethically right, this value can be counted as positive. The receiver's interpretation of a message and of the ensuing action are of fundamental importance in estimating both these values. (cf. Nissen 1983 and 1985) If every user of an information system shall be able to share the full responsibility for his/her action in the group, this has consequences for systems design. Then it is not sufficient to let the context of interpretation remain largely implicit. To support the receiver's interpretation, also historical and intentional contexts have to be explicitly expressed. This comprises contexts, including descriptions of work environments, both of the sender and of the receiver.

3.3 The standardization fiat used by data base designers

In the middle of the sixties, files of a data system became parts of a data base or became merged in a data base. At that time it was very important to gain advantages from the ´keen´ information in the whole organization, at low cost with the help of the computer. The information system service salesmen ´re-discovered´ an important resource of the enterprise. Besides work, material, capital and leadership, information became the fifth great resource of organizations. Centralization and standardization were very much the means in order to distribute this ´new´ resource to everyone ´who

needed it´, to everyone who was willing to pay for it, or
mostly to everyone in management who wanted to be in control
of part of the activities of an organization.

The ways of organizing the data in the base have followed
some main lines. The base unit in organizing a data base
could be a single abstract unnormalized relation, "the uni-
versal relation" (see Langefors 1963, Codd 1970 and Kent 1978
a.o.) or a concept of an entity in entity models (see Chen
1976). The base unit could also be some kind of relationship
between entities in functional models, networks or hierar-
chies. Another approach is the use of access-path models
which are based on sequential transformations (see Senko et
al 1973). ACM Computing Surveys (Sibley 1976) provide a forum
for several approaches, which might be of interest.

There have been a lot of necessary and good improvements made
in the data base field following the structuring logic and
semantic and the efficiency of the computerized system (see
e.g. Langefors & Sundgren 1975, Senko 1977, Kent 1978, Codd
1979, Ullman 1982 and Bubenko 1979 & 1983).

A very promising integration between the different approaches above and information structure is made by e.g. Sundgren
(1975). Date´s (1980) presentation of a unified language to
deal with common accessability, is another example of an
important integrating effort.

Data base designers use standards to map parts of reality
into a data base and the same or maybe other standards to
query the data base. What is done is to record some behol-
ders´ opinion about some part of reality, which at best is
an attempt to report objectively by means of a subjective
filter. (cf Sundgren 1973) This use of standards, however,
solves real life problems only to a limited extent. The
design of data bases has mainly been directed towards automa-

tic data processing, consistencies and compatibilities and
towards automatic processing and handling of texts.

In the 1960-s when the computer became a tool and a central
object for research, the fundamentally important social adap-
tion, in the context of human interaction, was often assigned
a secondary role at the best. The data base became the main
interest and formal logical thinking almost totally influenced
the design of the information system. Efficiency was the goal
and standards were common features in order to obtain it.

The above mentioned approaches do not take into account many
users´ differing points of view and intentions, their changing views over time and the differences between the sender´s
and the receiver´s contextual milieu. The data base designers
usually do not mention the action taken, based upon messages
mediated by a computerized information system.

It does not matter what kind of unit the designer has chosen
as a basis to represent reality in his data base, the result
has been a standard one, formed as designers logically represent phenomena. These forms will of course influence the data
base users and the results from the actions based upon the
messages from the data base. It is therefore important to
supplement data base research with research within the receiving and using realm on the receivers´ and users´ conditions. Scientists must place themselves inside the world
studied much more than they have done before.

When using standards, after a while we tolerate them, accept
them and at last we feel happy, i.e. we feel safe and un-
troubled abuot them (compare with "the golden section" in
art). But, maybe it is not the designers´ structures that
should be examples for standardization and, maybe a standardization, if any, should not be made for as many people.
Standardization could lead to an entropy phenomenon, where

there is nothing new permitted and everything becomes level-
led out or equalized. Even if it is not so drastic, data base
design and research might contribute to such a future without
complementary design and research.

Standardization is not often declared to have a steering
impact on purposes, actions and states, among data base
designers. But behind standards there is unconsciously or
consciously the intention to control (cf Berglind 1984) or
the need to feel secure. And if so, it is necessary at least
to expose the controlling function and illustrate how the
system has been constrained through this.

However, for quite a long time within economic research, our
attention has been drawn to the fact that there are dangers
with standards and normative (cf.e.g.Hayek 1937). De Monthoux
has studied the roles of rules, norms and maxims in industry.
His starting point has been the criticism that people are
unaware of the technical standardization and that they see
this as a result of something natural and not as something
artificial. He wants people to be conscious of the fact that
an implicit set of rules impact them and their actions. (cf.
de Monthoux 1981) Everybody must discover that they themselves can take part in developing artifacts for the world
they share with there fellowmen, for their purposes in reality. Thus possibilities for allowing many filters for several
perspectives in a data base have to be worked out.

3.4 The speech act as a new suit

Language is based on a set of norms. This fact has been used
by some information and computer researchers as a basis, in
their efforts to get closer to the nature of natural expressions and natural thoughts. I am here referring to the field
of artificial intelligence and particularly to the designers
of expert systems.

Many of them start from the speech act theory that was presented by Searle (1969). This theory emanates from Austin
(1962) and is an interpretation and development of Austin´s
ideas.

In the speech act theory, Searle makes distinctions between
different kinds of speech acts, such as utterance acts,
propositional acts and illocutionary acts. To give utterances to phenomena we employ morphemes and sentences. When
stating propositional acts we refer and predicate. Illocutionary acts are performed by stating, questioning, command-
ing, promising etc. (Searle p. 24)

The latter acts are then represented in the symbolic form,
F(p), where the variable "F" takes illocutionary force in-
dicating devices as values and "p" takes expressions for
propositions. Different illocutionary acts are then formed
$\vdash$ (p) for assertions, !(p) for requests, Pr(p) for promises,
W(p) for warnings and ?(p) for yes-no questions. These kinds
of representation forms are as made for computers and this
may be one of the reasons why it has become popular to use
speech act theory as a basis on which to build information
systems within artificial intelligence.

Speech act theory has also been used e.g. by Lyytinen,
Goldkuhl and Lehtinen to criticize ideas of traditional data
base theory (Lyytinen 1981; Goldkuhl & Lyytinen 1982;
Lyytinen & Lehtinen 1984) But by introducing these developed
types of speech acts, I do not think they help the users to
gain knowledge in order to present better arguments. It does
not help with stricter logics, as logical reasoning often
´misses the point´. Instead, a more fruitful approach also
permits substantive arguments. (cf. Toulmin 1958). Goldkuhl
and Lyytinen also say that they look on material acts 1) but
all their examples are just about speech acts, which belong

to "communicative acts" 1). They criticize atomic sentences but on the other hand they often treat speech acts out of a wider action context. (cf. Nissen 1984a)

Again we are confronted with a structured view of reality, but now the structures have got a new suit. Again deep analyses of sentences are undertaken outside their intentional or historical contexts and without action, in a broad sense, on the mediated messages. Here, it is important to distinguish symbolic actions, often but not always, performed as speech acts, and material actions. The latter comprise cases involving transformation or transportation of quantities of matter/energy of more than symbolic magnitude. Speech act theory presupposes an already established cultural convention. Examples of such acts are ´to sign an order´ and ´to get married´. In daily work in enterprises much verbal intervention is not conventionalized so strongly.

Austin (1962) uses the notion of perlocutionary acts (also mentioned by Searle 1969 p 25). These are correlated with the notion of illocutionary acts. They are consequenses or effects that such acts have on the actions, thoughts, or beliefs of hearers, receivers. For example "by arguing I may persuade or convince someone, by warning him I may scare or alarm him, by making a request I may get him to do somthing, by informing him I may convince him or get him to realize". The underlined expressions denote perlocutionary acts. (Searle 1969 p 25)

Somehow these latter acts have been foreseen as phenomena by designers using the speech act as an alternative. These acts are worth paying attention to when going further with promising approaches in other respects. Now they have become stereotyped, even if the results seem very natural by using the common sentence building or very intelligently, by using logical facilities when facing the use of the data system. How about the effects, the variations and free choices and what do people do? Instead, we need to start from a unity between language and reality. Israel (1982) argues that we cannot speak about things without speaking of possible actions and that we cannot speak about wishes, intentions and opinions without speaking of actions. The so called instrumental acts (Habermas 1979) are generally left out of the analyses. Sometimes they are just mentioned. The instrumental acts are contrasted with speech acts. 1) Still if no one else did the physical job, his/her managers would not be able "to do things with words". 2)

3.5 The single-sided meaning triangle

Most of the views mentioned on messages and information have hitherto been very close to formal language based on principles of logic.

However, at the beginning of this century there were attempts to explain in triads the meaning of a sign or a concept (Ogden & Richards 1923, Peirce 1931).

Ogden and Richards (1923) made a simple model which permits three different phenomena to be seen from the same point of view. They are illustrated by a diagram, the relations of thoughts (references), symbols (words) and referents (things) as they were found in reflective speech uncomplicated by emotional, diplomatic or other disturbances:

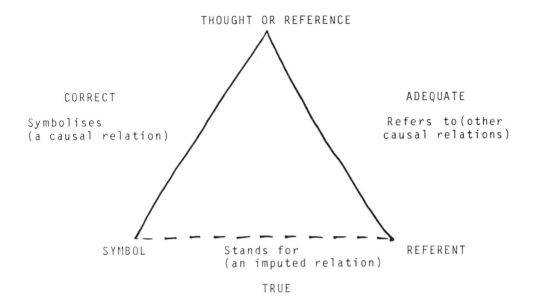

Figure 3.2: Ogden-Richards triangle (1923 p 11)

A symbol refers to what it is actually used to refer to; not
necessarily to what it ought to in good usage, or is intended
by an interpreter, or is intended by the user to refer to
(Ogden & Richards 1923 p 103). One symbol stands for one and
only one referent (ibid p 88). Symbols direct and organize,
record and communicate the thought. Symbols ´mean´ nothing
by themselves. They are instruments.

In figure 3.2 we have a diagram that shows a thought without
a thinker, a symbol without a maker, sender or receiver and a
referent that comes from nowhere. This is not a good explanation of conceptual meanings.

Instead, it is a very objectifying way of describing the
´meaning´ of a symbol. The ´meaning´ is not just a connection

of three entities. There are many more. It is also about the possibility to understand what has been said. There will be actions upon what has been said, independent of the message being true or false. The signs and the symbols themselves are social forces. The ´meaning´ of a word can more fruitfully be studied as a cultural entity. (Cf Eco 1971)

In spite of all these shortcomings, the above mentioned triangle is frequently used by system analysts and data base designers. (cf. e.g. Goldkuhl 1980 & Sowa 1984). That is my reason for mentioning it here.

A more fruitful proposal is the following, which borrows its features from Watzlawick (1967). It concerns relations between the sender and the reciever, the communication process, in which pragmatics is a behavioral affect. The sender and the receiver might belong to different places in space and time, have different contextual environments for the expressed phenomenon and have different intentions with the actual message. These four - space, time, environment and intention - are essential to me when studying ´meanings´. The Ogden-Richard triangle is delimiting and as Eco says (1971 p 62) it should leave place for a complicated polyeder. Such a polyeder cannot easily be represented on a flat paper, but here is an attempt:

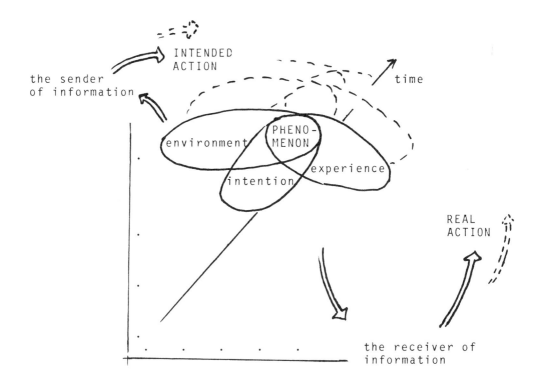

Figure 3.3: Pragmatics of phenomena in communication processes

Only relationships and patterns of relationships can be perceived as human experience, which is about a process of
change, motion and scanning. Functions, signs representing a
connection, are the essence of human experience. In inter-
personal systems you cannot always see what is energy, action
or gestures or.., and what is information. Sometimes they
appear at the same time. This is not the case when using
computers, if they are not parts of robots.

3.6 The sentence ´in vacuo´

It is not always enough with full sentences. Without their
context or presuppositions they will become sentences ´in

vacuo˝. The presuppositions in practice are usually not spoken or written ones. They are tacit and temporarily shared. The messages are dependent on their actual use. As Rommetveit (1974) says, there is an underlying conceptual reality. People may know something without being able to put it into words.

Langefors (1966) speaks about structural thinking within a system on a zero-intentional level. By using ˝message˝, apart from sentence, he permits himself to describe certain objects with certain characteristics, in a certain system at a certain time. There is no room for an intending message sender, any presuppositions, or for a quality description in the ˝message˝, which I following Ivanov (1972) will add to the message. I will also distinguish between an extensional and an intentional context of interpretation of the sentences exchanged.

Bubenko & Lindencrona-Ohlin (1984) a.o. describe possible external structures with the aim that they can be accepted by a computer, but they are talking about the importance of taking into account presuppositions. However, they speak about presuppositions hidden in data structures, not presuppositions in a person's mind when he informs somebody or is informed by somebody.

The contents rendered by such structures must be completed by specification of quality and by an intentional and a presupposing part i.e. by a quality dimension and contexts according to perspectives.

And - how about the intentional part? Does it exist? Yes, as an internal structure (maybe). In a committed form? No. Could we use some ˝natural logic˝ form to show such a form?

It might be fruitful to use the expressions, ˝intension˝, ˝intention˝ and ˝extension˝ as relational concepts, as in figure 3.4 below, between a sender, ANNA, and a receiver, PAUL, in order to avoid/detect sentences ´in vacuo´.

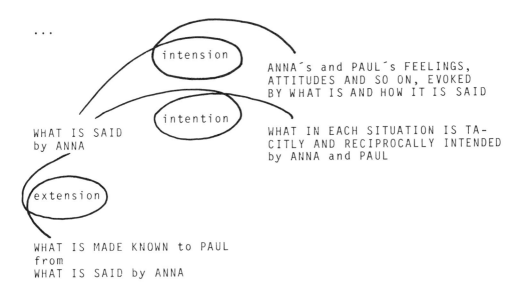

ANNA´s and PAUL´s FEELINGS, ATTITUDES AND SO ON, EVOKED BY WHAT IS AND HOW IT IS SAID

WHAT IS SAID
by ANNA

WHAT IN EACH SITUATION IS TA-CITLY AND RECIPROCALLY INTENDED by ANNA and PAUL

WHAT IS MADE KNOWN to PAUL
from
WHAT IS SAID by ANNA

Figure 3.4: Intentions, intensions and extensions as
relational concepts

Pragmatics concerns both what man really means, the intention, and how he manages to make something known to other people, in other words the extension. There exists also, the intension of a sentence, which means the feelings, attitudes and actions of the users, who were evoked by it. (cf. Rommetveit 1974)

Summary

In this chapter about present research, I have treated views on information and information systems and some approaches to design. I stressed the importance of the retrieving function in information systems and the present use of such systems.

The information concept has been treated from the point of quality and context. It is important to be aware of the fact that standards are both necessary and impressionable parts of our constructed social world. Speech act theory and Ogden´s triangle are not sufficient bases when modelling information systems. They must be completed by several perspectives from actors in order to avoid ´expressions out of context´ in informations systems.

Notes

1) Habermas (1979 p. 40) divides social actions into:
   instrumental actions
   symbolic actions (e.g. a concert, a dance, ...)
   communicative action, to which speech acts belong
   strategic actions.

2) The expression "to do things with words" I have borrowed from the title of Austin book on speech acts (1962).

4 Research Methods and Examples of Results

4.1 User and researcher participation

Within the research realms of information systems, there are people with quite different educational backgrounds and practical experience. Two main groups are ´the EDP specialists´ and ´the end users´. EDP specialists are well trained in systematic ordering and in setting up formal rules. Today their perspectives are mostly chosen to facilitate mechanization and computerization. When studying a computerized information system in use, their systematization already exists. Maybe the users want it redone after having detected, by themselves or supported by other people, a better way of using the system. This belongs to an active part of the learning and adaptive process.

The competence of an average end user of a computer is based on working life experience. The perspective is on various work tasks. The end-users also have their individual knowledge and their priorities and ways of solving problems. Therefore it is necessary in this research to work together with the end-users of the information systems. Methodologically and ideologically this is an urgent matter, as these people work with the system more or less continuously.

How my own participation and that of the end-users work, is illustrated below. The users´ experienced knowledge and skill and my scientific knowledge may together form new ways of problem finding and/or problem solving during the use of the system.

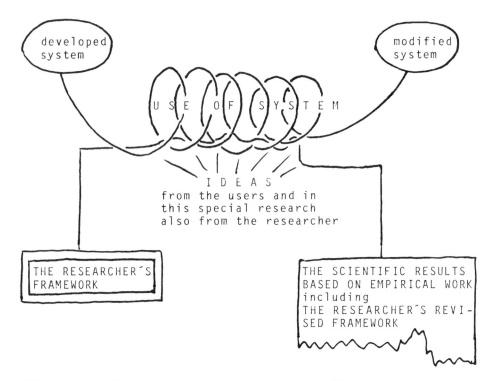

Figure 4.1: User and researcher participation when studying
the use of information system

The "developed system", the "USE OF SYSTEM" and the "modified
system" in figure 4.1, are the same as those in figure 1.2.
My presuppositions and other theoretical frames and guesses
about the practice, along with a ´plan of intervention´, are
the ingredients in the framework. The results are either new,
scientifically interesting questions, or contributions to an
information systems theory based on empirical work.

4.2 Intervening by the Sherlock Holmes´ method

Through my research I intend to support end-users, so that
they may acquire knowledge of new ways of action when using
information systems. This kind of research goal I cannot

achieve by only observing them as objects, the behaviour of which is to be predicted by deterministic or statistical general laws. Therefore, I have been using a learning and ´trying-out´ strategy, that I later on found to be most useful and hence, I have planned interventions for my empirical work.

This is in a way a necessity, in order to aid the users of the information system to get new ideas and to dare to take a chance to alter their use of the information system, or to develop and realize a new idea of their own.

I have to decide whether there are parts of my study that may be tackled in different ways with respect to the aim of my research. A great part of my study has methodological problems of a non-deterministic and non-stochastic character.

I need both quantitative and qualitative research methods. The quantitative methods are needed as preliminaries for qualitative methods and vice versa. I need both qualitative insight into the users´ real problems and quantitative overviews of general conditions. Qualitative insight and quantitative overviews may be achieved in parallel or interleaved. These kinds of integrated perspectives are shared with other researchers and good arguments for their use come from Grönmo (1984) and Tschudi (1984).

Interventions can be regarded as experiments that are not repeatable. In such experiments real important differences are apparent. Repeated experiments may be looked upon as special cases of interventions. They are characterized by (1) a high degree of control over the situation by the experimenter, (2) a decision to disregard as unimportant all remaining differences. I have made planned interventions in my empirical research in two organizations in order to get material, which cannot be gathered by traditional means.

The very first time it just happened. A great deal of my research work became fuel for discussing important things among the users about their work. As a researcher I became, without then knowing it, a very strong intervening factor as a result of earlier and/or hidden conflicts within one of the organizations. The conflicts were brought into light by me. These occurrences are intervening dilemmas worth noting for future researchers. Maybe what happens in such situations could lead to something good for the firms - so good that it is worth taking the risk of inviting a researcher.

Thanks to Dennett (1983), I have found out that what I have done methodologically, is that I have used similar tools to those of a detective. This method therefore is called "the Sherlock Holmes´ method", where by the intentional stance is a tool for generating or designing anecdotal circumstances (ibid pp 348-350).

Sherlock Holmes usually arranged traps and analogously I arranged for interventions. Sometimes I did it when I was not quite consciously aware of my intentions. Afterwards I observed the striking effects and therefore I tried a new similar intervention. Now it was more planned, based on earlier experience. Beforehand, some conjecture and one or more counter-conjectures and expectations were needed as to what outcomes of the intervention corroborate the one or the other. Ideally, the users should form these conjectures and criteria for deciding between them. The method is, of course, especially, effective in such situations, where the anecdotes could be generated several times under similar conditions.

From these interventions and often planned situations, I strove to secure permanent traces. In these I tried to find a pattern, useful for the users of the systems studied, for other users, for myself and my contemporaries in research and education.

4.3 The hermeneutic helix

My work should be seen as a learning process in order to gain further insight into information and information systems, from their uses in practice. This learning process has similar features to the hermeneutic helix, which is essentially a very general model of the development of knowledge through a tacking procedure or dialectics. The perspectives are the same as those in the two important processes ´systems development´ and ´systems use´. From the users´ problems, or the bad symptom of the information system in a rather fuzzy description, a possible solution can be suggested that may not be a satisfactory one. However, from this solution it may be possible to clarify the basic problem and reach a new solution that is more satisfactory than the first one, and so on, until sufficient remedies are achieved for the problem. Not before this point has the problem been satisfactorily defined. During this spiral process, more and more knowledge is accumulated about the context and the history of the problem and the users´ purposes in using the information system.

The research process contains conscious interventions. It follows rather closely a research design presented by Susman and Evered (1978).

The main steps in the research process, illustrated below, can be repeated several times, hopefully improving and understanding knowledge of information and information system use. (See also Nissen et al. 1982)

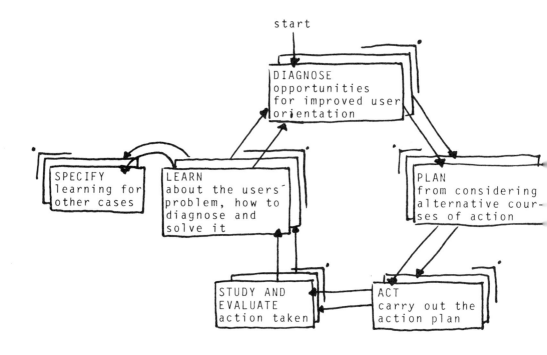

Figure 4.2: Development of the client organization
infrastructure in a research process

This so called action research process is recommended by
Järvinen (1984) for application and problem-solving tasks,
which both exist in my research.

4.4 How to generalize knowledge

From several learning processes on the same theme, it may be
possible to generalize from a certain moment, after the study
and evaluation phase. When we have used a planned intervening
research process, there is a fully realistic possibility of
accumulating knowledge to achieve a higher degree of generalization. In empirical work, I think this is a very useful
way of saving traces and patterns that could be seen, in some
aspects as being generally useful in other cases. Generaliza-

tion, however always means consciously ignoring differences
between the cases. Therefore it seems important to state explicitly for each theory, which differences have been ignored.

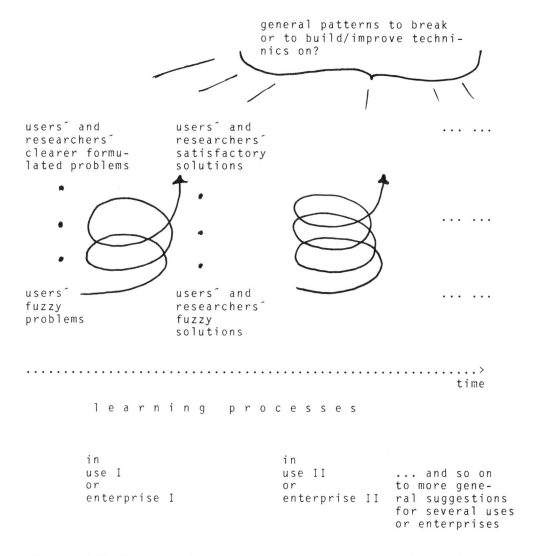

Figure 4.3: To generalize from learning processes in social
            research

Permanent traces of the processes, I studied and tried to
learn about, were saved - for me, people in the field of

study and other researchers - in order to reflect upon and interpret and re-interpret later on. These interpretations may result in identifying patterns of some kind. For these patterns it makes sense of asking if they are to be continued or broken.

4.5 Plans for empirical work

In the different enterprises, I had to inform the people I was going to work with, my intentions with the research and what they could expect from me during my stay at the places of work. Therefore in order to keep some kind of check on myself, I made some plans, one for each place of work. The plans were based on the same principles and ideas and here I am showing just one of them as an example. I am taking the one that concerns some departments of the manufacturing company.

For them and a few departments within two other organizations, I worked out and presented a plan for the users of my common investigation of their information system. The plan contains six phases, which are named according to the main activities that took place within each phase:

		User Time	Researcher Time
★	introducing	15	5
★	observing	2	40
★	participating	3	10
★	explaining	45	30
★	free telling and	10	20
★	evaluating activities.	30	20

The time devoted, in man hours, to each phase for the users and myself, are indicated in the columns. The figures are avarage for the five areas studied. The figures do not include time for discussions among the users afterwards, as a result of my visits, for travels or for documentation.

I   The introducing phase:

Here, I wanted to know in what environment an information system was working and also wanted to get acquainted with the users and tell them about myself and my intention concering my working with them.

I wanted to establish working situations that can exist as a result of questions of the following kinds, that I put to myself and to which I looked for answers from personal contact with the users. The questions were also asked directly and got direct answers. The questions in this phase were like the following ones, though re-worded according to the situation:

* What is your actual job?
* What different situations occur during your work?
* From where do the decision bases come?
* To whom is the result delivered?
* Whom does the user help?
* What kind of problems are solved?
* How are the decision bases put together?
* From where does the basic information come?
* Is the working situation team-oriented and in that case who is in the team?
* Is the information system used and in that case for what and why or respectively, why not?

Morover I wished to find out the total number of users and their function
- professionally
- in relation to the information system,
   that is if they were terminal users, system users, ´ser-
      vers´, decision makers, executives and so on ...
   or if they were ´data feeders´ or ´data needers´ or both.

This introducing phase was mostly devoted to finding out what the users were doing, their work as a whole, their different working situations, the special working situations concerning their information system, where they wanted support from their own system, the intentions with their searching for information, what problems they were solving and whom they thought they were helping. Some of the results have already been presented in section 1.4.

II   Observing phase:

The physical use of their ´own´ information system was the object of my observation. I found it important to describe how the users actually and practically worked by
- seeing and interpreting myself what they were doing
- asking and listening to what they thought they were doing with the help of the information system.

III   Participating phase:

Participation on my part, was necessary in order to make possible an increased understanding of what the users were doing. This was disclosed by how they spoke about their work, and what they took for granted when speaking about it. This was also very important methodologically for my research, from which I wanted to learn how others understand their world. Therefore it was necessary to learn their jargon and way of speaking, to become familiar with some of the concepts that stand for important phenomena in their work and that are mediated by their information bank or data bases.

The order between the observing phase and the participating phase was sometimes altered or mixed.

IV   Explaining phase:

The users were given the task of explaining to me as an outsider, some concepts that I had gathered during earlier parts of my investigation. The time given for answering was two hours. The tasks had the following form:

"Explain to me - as an outsider - the following concepts/words/expressions in some simple sentences. If you are feeling unfamiliar with the words then write "I do not understand". If you know that you have met the concept earlier and that it no longer means anything to you, then write what fits best - "meaningless" or "forgotten"."

The investigation of some concepts was supplemented with questions such as:
* How do you use the concept?
* Why do you use the concept?
* In which situations do you use the concept?

This part was carried out simultanously by use of questionnaires (see appendix A) by individuals from a larger group doing the same kind of work. They were working in adjacent rooms, when they filled in the questionnaires. The number of concepts was about 20. In order to avoid time pressure followed by hasty answers, I dared not test with too many concepts at a time.

In one of the investigations, I had to repeat this phase orally in smaller groups using new concepts, as I had become too much of an intervening factor when trying to do this with paper and pencil. The users had felt like controlled objects and many of them refused to participate as I had intended them to do. In this case, when orally repeated, I used ´the inquiry method´ by Postman and Weingartner (1969) as shown in section 4.6.

V   Free telling phase:

The users tell me about the use and the non-use of their own systems and other information sources by answering the following kinds of questions:

What is the best and the worst thing about your own system? ... with other sources? Did you participate in the development of the system? When was the system developed? How did you learn to use the system? When did you start using the system? Did you ever contribute to improving the system?

These questions were put into the other phases when it was suitable. The questions were not given to all the employees in the department, even if I met most all of them, 25 people in the actual manufacturing case. The replies and knowledge about the person who could answer the questions, completed my image of the users´ backgrounds and their possibilities of influencing their own working situation with respect to computerized information systems. I am not using the answers to traditionally classify the users, but rather to get a background when studying the interpretations and actions on phenomena mediated by their information system. I had to have these contexts, as well as what I perceived from phase I, for my studies.

VI   Evaluating phase:

By Osgood´s semantic differential (Osgood et al. 1967) I made an evaluation on the basis of the user´s opinions in a diagram (see appendix D and section 5.7) concerning
- computer display language
- computer based decision support
- their computer
- professional knowledge after acquiring their data system
- their work after acquiring their data system

in order to find some common positive or negative attitudes to the use of computerized information systems. See the following section 4.7 about this measuring method.

On the whole, I have followed the structure expressed by the six phases above. Most importance has been attached to the explaining and evaluating phases. The other phases are merely needed to execute these two important phases in practice.

4.6 A method of inquiry

As a method questioning a person about things that I do not know much about in advance. I used an idea given to me by Postman & Weingartner (1969). They were using it for teaching purposes.

I have used their idea in my investigation of the use of information and information systems. I also think this method is very useful when trying to change the structure of the systems development situation. I mean that this way of interviewing people is radically different, from the average or normal one, which makes it possible for people to activate their minds, attitudes and comprehension.

Instead of starting to ask about figures, labels and values, I asked for functions, intentions and importance. Instead of trying to cover the content of what is going on, I wanted the users to tell me about their important ideas, problems and opinions. The questions must open the ability to think both for the users and myself. The hermeneutic helix must not be rigidly planned in the same sense as the planned sequence of a formal education. The helix is not an instrument to follow slavishly. The quantitive material I gathered afterwards on the same or a later occasion. Much of the quantitative material is documented already and is rather easily gatheredin

the users´ own report on statistics, which they have been
told to make by law and superiors.

An example concerning the inquiry method:
I do not start asking for   I am asking for
"How many transactions..?"   "How does the information system
                                 take care of transactions"

"Of what parts does the   "How does this system work?"
 system consist?"

"Is this system good or.."   "Why is this system important?"
    .   .
    .   .

For real questions see appendix C.

I have tried to find questions that activate the users´ minds
and get them to the point of emancipating: "Maybe this could
be changed... .". I think they told me much more about their
problems and ideas, but the real point is that they - maybe I
can say - ´spontaneously´ came to think about them at all.

The aim of this method of inquiry is to support a person
   * to raise his ability to learn and act
   * to get rid of the distrust of originality
   * to believe in his ability to improve and
   * to realize that problem solving is something to enjoy.
The method helped both the users and myself. If people are
allowed by management to do something about their work situation, i.e. really change if they feel a need, is of course of
the greatest importance here. Whether this was the case in
the situations in question was not always easy to get a clear
opinion of.

When using this method in a group of people, one question
probably gives several answers. The opinions from several
people may be gathered. The questions give the group more new
ideas in total from the answers and counter-questions. The

quality of the users´ ideas should not be judged and no
summary should be made during the interviews, so that the
discussions not will be interrupted.

I can give some examples to show how it works. There is a
situation involving diagnostic work and I am discussing with
a few diagnosticians some expressions that they use daily
in their reference answers or suggestions for such answers.
The first example is about ´finding or not-finding any malignant cells´-situation in the microscopic picture of a sample
from a ´feeling-ill´-woman´s mammae. The ´concept´ discussed
was "the cell picture". The answers to the two questions "Are
you worried when the cell picture is regular?" and "Are you
worried when the cell picture is irregular?" These two questions are very important for the patient, the diagnostician,
and the clinical doctor as well, as you will soon understand.
The investigation, through the two questions, gave the following result:

A positive answer (a "yes" or an implicit "yes") to the first
question may mean two things according to those who were
asked. Either the diagnostican is worried about taking the
responsibility of the diagnosis "regular cell picture", i.e.
that the patient does not have cancer, or the diagnostican is
worried that just this regularity could indicate a special
kind of cancer, but he/she can not see it. A negative answer
to the first question may signify that they feel sure about
the diagnosis "nothing malignant" that follows upon a "regular cell picture" or they do not feel worried because the
client is not that ill.

A positive answer to the second question may indicate, still
according to those people being asked, that the diagnostician feels for the client that is really sick and a negative
answer could imply that the diagnostician is sure of his/her
diagnosis. It is easier to be sure about a malignant diagno-

sis than about a benign diagnosis.

To these two, and all the other, questions there were ˉpositive˘, ˉnegative˘ and ˉit depends onˉ answers and during the discussion they also came with counter-questions and changed their opinions. Thus, there is much behind the expressions ˉregular cell picture˘ and ˉirregular cell picture˘ of importance for the patient the diagnostician and, of course, for the receiver, the clinical doctor who should help the patient to recover from a cancer or from the chock of the message or help the patient to live with the knowledge of a lethal threat.

The material in this kind of investigation will be developed for research and systems use, on the basis of the usersˉ reaction and not so much on the logical structure that had been made beforehand. Success is measured with the help of the actions and/or expressed wishes of the users of the information system.

Similar discoveries have been made by Lanzara and Mathiassen (1984 p. 37):

"In many respects the logic of intervention differs from the logic of analysis. It limelights and focuses on the situations as they are experienced by the actors: systems, functions, procedures, and technical equipment are not just wiped out as irrelevant, on the contrary they are necessary elements of the actorsˉ situation contributing to shape it, but they lay - so to speak - in the background of the situation."

4.7 Measurement by Osgoodˉs semantic differential

The questions in the explaining phase are value-questions of another kind than the remaining ones in the investigation. I will use a well frequented method called "the semantical differential" to collect and analyze people´s opinions about their work and their computerized information systems. I do this for two reasons. One, is that I wish to try an ordered quantitative method that is combined with measuring quality values to see how it works. The other is that I wish to know the users´ opinions, through an anonymous investigation within the work group.

"The semantic differential is a method of observing and measuring the psychological meaning of concepts." (Kerlinger 1964, p 566) In all concepts there must be some common core of meaning. Osgood invented the semantic differential to measure the connotative meanings of concepts as points in what he has called ´semantic space´ (Osgood, et al. 1957).

A semantic differential consists of a number of scales, each of which is a bipolar adjective pair. The bipolar adjectives are usually seven point rating scales, where the underlying nature has to be determined empirically. In my research I have clustered the bipolar pairs into evaluation and potency adjectives. I have chosen my own pairs of adjectives for this investigation (see appendix D) based upon an intuitive and experienced knowledge of ´users and their data systems´.

To illustrate the method, I choose the following example. In a working group in a department, the members were asked to fill in five forms about different concepts regarding their own work. One of the forms concerns the "computer display language". I asked them to associate spontaneously with "computer display language", something between the following pair of evaluating and action-related adjectives:

```
inexact         :_____:_____:_____:_____:_____:_____:   exact

rich            :_____:_____:_____:_____:_____:_____:   poor
incompre-                                               intelli-
hensible        :_____:_____:_____:_____:_____:_____:   gible

entertaining    :_____:_____:_____:_____:_____:_____:   boring

correct         :_____:_____:_____:_____:_____:_____:   invalid

fragmentary     :_____:_____:_____:_____:_____:_____:   complete
                                                        full of
stereotyped     :_____:_____:_____:_____:_____:_____:   nuances

fuzzy           :_____:_____:_____:_____:_____:_____:   clear

angular         :_____:_____:_____:_____:_____:_____:   flexible

wrong           :_____:_____:_____:_____:_____:_____:   correct
```

Figure 4:4: Form for measuring opinions on display language

The results obtained are then grouped according to kinds of
end-users and to closely related adjectives for presentation
and discussion. This will be shown in section 5.7.

Summary

The methods used in the empirical work emanate from learning
perspectives that are of the greatest importance when trying
to make interventions, so that the end-user may see ways to
modify or new ways of using his information system. A plan
for the investigations undertaken is presented and also methods of inquiry and evaluation to find out the users' opinions of their work and their computerized supporting system.

5 Understanding Phenomena from Practical Life

The use of information systems is an ongoing learning process. The search for knowledge functions as a hermeneutic
spiral (Radnitzky 1970), where every curve in the spiral
gives the user more and more knowledge about the problems in
question and the solutions. This whole amount of knowledge is
achieved through interactions between the information system
and its users, who each have their own previous experience
and their own evaluations as contributions. The users´ problems in their daily work and their way of finding satisfactory solutions can be described as follows.

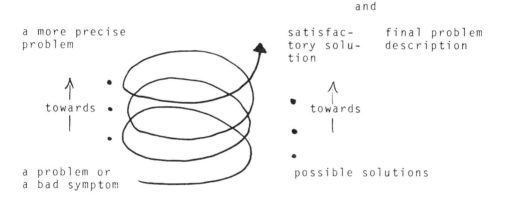

Figure 5.1: Problem solving as a learning process

This is a similar kind of phenomenon for research work (cf
section 4.3) and as it should be for systems development (cf.
Höyer 1979). However, there is not that sharp awareness of
the learning process as in research activities advocating the
process itself. Therefore I am just describing the problem
finding and solving part.

Very often, the users may not know how good a solution is and what the problem really looks like. This is a somewhat secret knowledge. The spiral in the figure above is open. The problem is not very hard structured. Another way of expressing this is through ´tacit knowledge´ (Polanyi 1966 p. 3-25). ´Tacit knowledge´ is non-tangible and personal knowledge and it will stay that way. The belief that, since small parts are very tangible in detail (visible loose rose petals) they are carrying true knowledge about the whole (the rose), is wrong. If we take away the tacit knowledge, there will be no perfect rose. There will be no efficient problem solving either. As an illustrative example from my empirical work I want to describe the following case.

A cythologic diagnostician said to me while working: "I know that this is cancer. I so badly want to find malignant cells. Sometimes the cells are piled up when the specimen is taken and they are formed in a special way. Sometimes you getunusually many benign cells as a result of this in a specimen. It happens that the background of the specimen gives a malignant impression, that is how I know that this is cancer, but I can´t find just one malignant cell, so I have to write "no malignant cells" in the space for cythologic diagnosis on the note of admission." In this particular case the patient had cancer and this was diagnosed later on through other methods too and she got the appropriate treatment.

One doctor wanted the diagnoses papers to ´breathe´ what they were about. I think this is a conscious statement about the importance of tacit knowledge. People in laboratories want their tacit results forwarded to clinical doctors in order to raise the quality of medical care. Thus, they want their tacit knowledge both to seem hard and to remain tacit. But if

the tacit results are not expressed, then they cannot be
forwarded, or if they are expressed then they do not remain
tacit. This is a dilemma that cannot be solved by computers.

I can speak here about personal intuitive knowledge and human
experienced knowledge. When speaking about a skilled person,
it is the ability, or inability, to do certain things that
counts. It is more to know how to play an instrument than
know that something is the case. I think of Ryle´s pair of
"knowing that and knowing how", by which he understands the
following:

> "In ordinary life...we are much more concerned with peop-
> le´s competences than with their cognitive repertoires,
> with the operations (knowing how) than with the truths that
> they learn (knowing that). ... To be intelligent is not
> merely to satisfy criteria, but to apply them; to regulate
> one´s actions and not merely to be well-regulated." (Ryle
> 1949 pp. 28-29; my parentheses)

The concept ´experienced knowledge´ is also frequently used
by Göranzon and Josefsson in their results from empirical
works. They define ´experienced knowledge´ as consisting of
collected experience, acquired after a long period of work
within the realm of the knowledge. It is the collected result
of failures and corrections, wrong decisions and changed
opinions, which in the end function. (Göranzon 1978, Göranzon
& Josefson 1980)

In ´real´ problem solving there is always a moment of intuition. Otherwise we know what we are looking for and then
there is in reality no problem at all. In ´real´ problem
solving there is also almost always a moment of experience.
Otherwise we could not get any contextual background to the
problem and it is difficult to detect and explain.

Thus, during "towards a more precise problem" and "towards a satisfactory solution" (see figure 5.1) there are also contributions of ideas. It is through action that we finally solve or dissolve a real problem. As a data processing specialist I must not disregard this.

"to see a problem is to see something that is hidden"

This is said by Polanyi (1966 p. 21). He has a narrower definition of the concept ´problem´ than that of the data processing specialists. Their wider definition can then be said to also involve problems with solutions, which are easy to see. We should, however, be aware of the danger of pushing the problem solving too far with the support of data systems. We should not analyze roses to death by tearing off the petals in order to examine them. We must learn to stop in time.

5.2 Intuitive, rational and empirical knowledge

A rhythmical, cyclic changing between freedom of action and discipline should also be the aim in our daily work in order to find good solutions to problems. Alternating ideas, precision and generalizing phases are often the conditions of a good psychological working situation and of a thoroughly penetrated task. Most jobs require moments of creativity, where we cannot omit or forget that the idea phase is justified. The novelty ´the idea´, is built on intuition and on combinations with intuition.

From the integral knowledge theory of Sorokin (1941 p. 762-763) it is said that there are many ways of reaching knowledge. He concerns himself with three fundamental channels to acquire it:
* experienced knowledge is gained through our senses and their extensions as e.g. tools in daily work

* rational knowledge is gained through our intellect, through
  our mathematical and logical thinking
* intuitive knowledge, such as insight, inspiration and creativity.
The three ways of acquiring knowledge, complement, rectify and
balance each other (Lindholm 1983).

The three ways of acquiring knowledge are also needed to
solve tasks in daily work, even for tasks, where a computer
is involved. I mean that the human being as a whole requires
this, even if he does not say so explicitly. The expressed
requirement in an organization also leads to the conclusion
that it is not enough with empirical and rational knowledge.
The individual man and the overall organization, may both
gain through better decision making and better decision exe-
cution by means of supplementary knowledge. By letting the
learning process work on a wider knowledge basis, within a
more informally organized team and with the same main working goal, I believe it will be possible to come closer to a
better work process and a better work result. This hypothesis
is backed up by McGregor (1960) and his Y-theory, where he
assumes that people take the initiative, are responsible and
are active without being told to be so. The theory Y implies
that effectivness will be high when authority and communication flow in both formal and informal systems and when work
is varied and enriched.

It is important to give people every chance to act indepen-
dently and thus individuals gain self-fulfillment and the
organization gains a better performed job, for example better
medical care. However, it is always difficult to reorganize
and to find the proper size of team with contributing participants whose individual talents and capacities must be ca-
tered for. At least, we must not have information systems as
intentional obstacles in these matters.

Sorokin (1941) suggests that many qualitative aspects of the phenomena that we perceive through our senses, are inaccessible to us when only using logical-mathematical thinking. Such quality aspects are also inaccessible to the kind of structural thinking that is reflected in data bases. If such aspects are involved in a daily work situation, it seems reasonable not to let computers entirely control this work. I suggest that it should be the people who do the work that should decide to a great extent, when it is wise to accept support from a data system.

This contributes to concurrence with intuition, logic and experience. Such a three-dimensional system of knowledge is needed even when using computers. It is even necessary if we do not want to penetrate the essence of the world with very little intuition. The meaning of this could result in aconflict between structural thinking and wisdom even in quite an ordinary job. If this conflict is won by logic through high computerization we might soon end up with a kind of entropy of structure beyond the reach of intuition. To avoid such a conflict there must be room for all these three channels to produce knowledge.

5.3 Sediment of history

In the organizations I am studying, there are rem(a)inders from information system development work performed in the sixties and seventies. Traces of a highly structured information system in expert codes are extremely common. They exist as sediment in the organization. Sediment is the result of the inherent human institutions. They are without real functions and normally tend to persist until they become problematic. (cf. Berger & Luckmann 1966, Danielsson 1975). It is as if a law of inertia ruled.

Sediment also appears in the method of application and in systems design. The old ways of thinking concerning old-fashioned equipment are still alive in new development. It does not matter to what extent the work is done with the help of the users. There also exists sediment of relations between the system users and the data experts.

Empirically I have found a lot of examples of such sediment. They are visible at places of work, where the work is diminishing and where there is no requirement for profit centre responsibility. At one place, there was, in practice, just one person who was using a computerized information system. This system user recieved about 15 long lists of information every month from the data system and he made real use of only three of them. This phenomenon has remained from the good years of this department, when there was a need for all the lists. Lists produced in batches are themselves another example of sediment. And when I asked the user why he did not do anything about it, he said that it was not his business; that should be decided by the designer and those who decide about the money. These statements are also examples of sediment. I did not imagine before my studies that it would be possible to meet that kind of old-fashioned way of thinking in practice.

In the 1960s, the human interpretations of signs and sentences in the files were represented atomically in structured records. There was a very simple interface between the users and the files. The files gave the users their results, aggregated from separate facts named from a hierarchy. The results came out from a strictly controlled distribution phase on pyjama-striped sheets of paper.

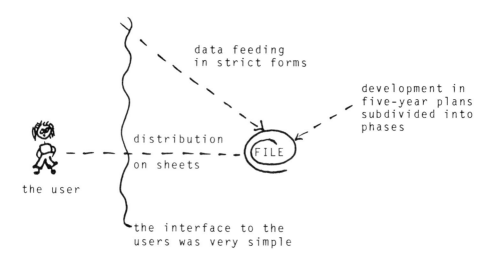

data feeding
in strict forms

development in
five-year plans
subdivided into
phases

distribution
on sheets

FILE

the user

the interface to the
users was very simple

Figure 5.2: Use and development in the 1960s

In the 1970s the situation improved but it has not caught
up with technology. The data base was still an artifact that
was not on a level with the requirements. These grew more and
more and there were many separate files on the same and also on
different topics and still a lot of sorting and merging. The
systems were both large and ´small in networks´. The requirements concerning the quality of data became more important
and the result was more formal technique, large scale production of technology, computer networks and security codes.

The data base design and technique gave the user several
possibilities to combine the stored atomic data or stored
atomic sentences. The total flatness of the files was changed
into more dimensions. From the atoms more and more elements
were synthesized, i. e. more and more data were aggregated.
The technological advances were great at the end of 1970s.

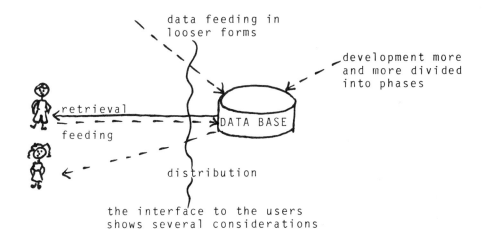

Figure 5.3: Use and development in the 1970s

In the 1980s the data base gets several ´colours´, i.e. that different perspectives from the users are allowed. It should be natural that systems development ´in the small´, runs pa-rallel to systems use. Rather complex interfaces are possible in view of technological progress, that allow considerably more individual possiblities for the users. Systems develop-ment should take place all the time in view of the working situation.

Data bases are becoming more and more sophisticated and at the same time people are becoming more aware of the possibi-lities and dangers with computers. They can be used almost in any field of industry and administration, but the rigidity of computers is still there to a great extent.

Computers and data bases should function more as a supplement rather than as the only source of knowledge for any profes-sion. Within all systems development, the work situation should be studied first.

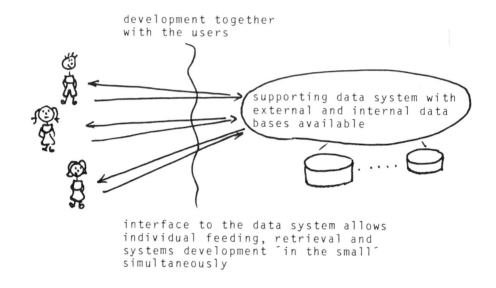

development together
with the users

supporting data system with
external and internal data
bases available

interface to the data system allows
individual feeding, retrieval and
systems development ´in the small´
simultaneously

Figure 5.4: Use and development in the 1980s

Both use and development are of course influenced by earlier
experience of information systems. Old habits are deep-
rooted. It is hard to get rid of old habits and it is not
always easy to think that changes are good ones. This is
valid also as far as meanings of expressions are concerned.
They may not be permitted to change the meaning or ´to change
their owner´. It is difficult for an old ´data base digger´
to think in these terms.

5.4 Association problems

Every human being associates with earlier knowledge when
thinking. They associate in several steps, levels and or
directions very rapidly. This process is very hard to de-

scribe in a logical way and thus associative and flexible descriptions from human thinking are next to impossible to express in data bases. There are no rules, constraints, or limits to follow. Such descriptions could be connections between entities from a line of choice. Associations seem to be formed through different kinds of similarities.

In one organization, I came across the expression ´biopsy´ and this expression was orally defined in an investigation by several people in quite different ways. In spite of my belief that they were all very well acquainted with ´biopsy´, the expression was defined as: "a little piece", "the opposite to autopsy" "splitting of living material", "part of living material", "laboratory", "sample piece", "secretary station at the pathology", "cutting from living people", "seeing living material", "looking at living samples", "pieces of living materia", "microscopy" a. o. These meanings are all the kind of associations that belong to the experience from the real biopsy and from the word ´biopsy´ itself. How the meanings really have been formed is mostly very hard to prove.

Somebody has seen the prefix ´bi-´ and transformed this in some way. Another person has seen the prefix ´bio-´ and thought of ´..living..´. Some have seen the suffix ´-sy´ and hear inside themselves ´see´ as a kind of synonym. They then go further to ´look at´. Others rather think of ´-opsy´ and so on. Many combinations exist and there are also interpretations based on daily experience, such as that there are secretaries working in the biopsy team and that the people interviewed had themselves done biopsy work. All of the people interviewed except one doctor, with a so called correct dictionary explanation ("looking at living material"), had many associations and gave several definitions before they decided on just one. This is a confirmation that the meaning of an expression easily becomes a new one, even when it comes from the same person.

These hinted association tracks could be set up in a structure as relations between entities from some chosen line. Associations can be developed through different kinds of similarities in form and meaning or in one of the two. It can concern suffix, prefix or other parts of the expressions that are similar all the time. It can also be founded on synonymous expressions. See figure 5.5 below.

All these definitions were really intended to explain to me as an outsider what the expression ´biopsy´ means. For this reason they used their belief of what I wanted to hear and of what I possibly knew and of who I am. These possibilities do not very often exist when talking through a computer. The receiver is too anonymous, a researcher, a clinician, a secretary, an assistant, not Anderson or Smith exactly. The receiver may also be the sender himself/herself in several years time.

These kinds of lines for choice in the thinking process cannot be represented, but they exist in the layer between semantics and pragmatics and must be seen as part of the communication process and as such they have to be noticed. The limitations of a data system became apparent in this matter.

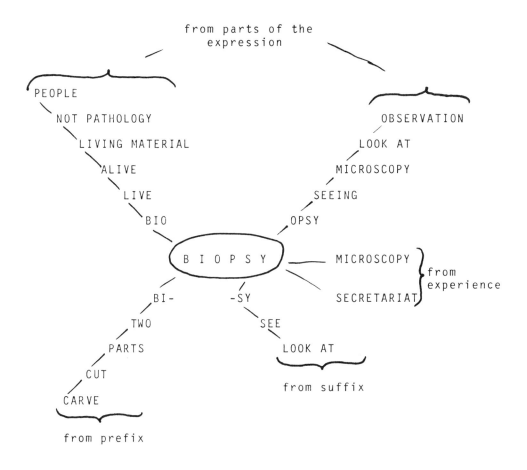

Figure 5.5: Different association tracks based on synonym and linguistic choices

To catch such multivalences is to catch meanings important for the enterprise and only the users can offer them. But most likely most of the meanings cannot be found at one go during a system development phase. Still, several meanings will most likely be mentioned by the users, whereas only one will generally be documented as the correct and only one for the limited purpose at that time. Later, data from the same system may be used in other contexts.

5.5 Strengthening and weakening words

By reading references on patients at a hospital I understood that small words could have a decisive effect upon the treatment of the patient. With a great deal of vital support from a cythological doctor and diagnostician, I started an investigation about strengthening and weakening words taken from real diagnoses. This investigation was not planned from the beginning of my research at the hospital. It was the result of a need from the users of the information system to know if these little words did any harm or good. It was of great interest to find out whether these words have any effect on the receiver - the clinical doctor. We wanted to know if he/she did different things if the diagnosis was strengthened or weakened by the help of some small words such as

serious	medium hard	slight
severe	moderate	gentle
strong	modest	faint
hard		

In work where everything is done manually and where one could discuss mutually, the parties concerned may come to the conclusion that they mean the same, or that they do not mean the same with such a word. In teamwork, this may work very well. They get used to each other and learn to use the same expressions. They might also agree on which word should be used in a certain case. All of them also give almost the same meaning to an expression, if it concerns a piece of work that all of them see and act within, i.e. to the extent they communicate about a shared reality (cf. Berger & Luckman 1966, Rommetveit 1974). Such teamwork situations are not common in today's hospital work in Sweden. Medical care is specialized and controlled centrally.

Imagine any of the above-mentioned words in an information system followed by the word "cancer". Furthermore, imagine that the working realm is alive but concerns sick people, or is important medical research. Also, imagine that one person orders another to put into the system a diagnosis, that will be taken out of the system much later or will be taken out by another person in order to compare it with research material. It may even be removed in order to operate on or to prescribe the treatment of a sick human being. There are a lot of reasons to think over what can be done.

The investigation was carried out on questionnaires in two sets, somewhat different from each other. The questionnaires and the results are presented in appendix B. Here some plans and results of the investigation are shown.

There were 19 clinical doctors, 19 diagnosticians, and 10 language experts who were asked to rank some expressions containing words such as "suspected, probable and possible". The doctors were those who received the stated opinions from the diagnosticians. The language experts were scientists from different faculties.

To be more exact theywere asked to rank the following:
"malignancy cannot be excluded"
"strong suspicion of malignancy"
"malignancy cannot be entirely excluded"
"suspicion of malignancy"
"some suspicion of malignancy"

and to rank the following
"most likely cancer"
"possibly cancer"
"probably cancer"

Some people were asked to interpret these two stated opinions:
"Most likely cancer of type A"
"Cancer, most likely cancer of type A"
and some other people were asked to interpret the following statement:
"Most likely cancer of type A"
"Possibly cancer of type A"
"Probably cancer of type A"

The investigation was carried out in Sweden and in Swedish, and the material is now translated into English and in connection with this, it might have been changed somewhat in the interpretation.

I have chosen the expressions, used in the investigation, together with a doctor, who daily makes diagnoses of cancer cells and who has initiated the coding to the local data system in use. The codes are in these matters planned to be based on the "System Information Qualifiers" (see appendix B) from the "Systemized Nomenclature of Medicine - microglossary for surgial pathology" (SNOMED 1980). You will there find the qualifiers for certainty of diagnosis. Another source in these matters is the references, where I found the expressions which have been studied.

The most common rankings found in the references among the different respondents are the following:

	doctors	diagnos-ticians	language experts
Replying (consulted)	18 (19)	15 (19)·	9(10)
Number of these replies	8	4	5
	the rankings		
malignancy cannot be excluded	2	2	2
strong suspicion of malignancy	5	4	5
malignancy cannot be entirely excluded	1	1	1
suspicion of malignancy	4	3	4
some suspicion of malignancy	3	1	3

Interesting, however, are not the similarities but the differences. The rest of the replies from the doctors were all,
with one exception, different from each other. The most odd
answer was the one which contained the opinion that "strong
suspicion" and "suspicion" was of the same severity, ranked
as 2 each, and somewhat more severe than the others, all
ranked as 3.

Six more rankings other than that typical for the diagnosticians appeared and the most odd was the non-ranking one. It
contained just one figure, the 1. My interpretation of this
message is that this person did not find my investigation
worth a thourough answer and that he wanted to demonstrate
it. Another interpretation is that this person did not find
any reason to distinguish between the expressions when writing the diagnoses.

Several language experts agreed about the same ranking as
several doctors. These two categories were both very highly
educated compared to the diagnosticians. However, the rest of
the doctors had one opinion each.

The most common ranking of some certainty qualifiers within
medicine is as follows:

	doctors	diagnos-ticians	language experts
Replying (consulted)	18 (19)	15 (19)	9(10)
Number of these replies	9	3	4
most likely cancer	3	2	3
possibly cancer	1	1	1
probably cancer	2	2	2

Here, ´possibly´ was the most vague word throughout the
investigation. Just in two cases it was equal to the others.

This was just an investigation and the consulted were aware
of that and they had seen the alternatives at the same time.
In reality, they almost always had just one of the expressions, before their eyes, and the situation is not the same
with an expression isolated for absolute judging as it is
with an expression related to other similar expressions.

Except the main meanings from the different groups, the re-
mainder, practically everybody, had different opinions.

The interpretations in their own words about ´most likely cancer
of type A´ were the following
from the doctors

I
"not definitely diagnosted cancer"
"not definitely malignancy diagnosis"
"cancer of type A until the opposite has been proved"
"malignancy, that should be discussed"
"not a certain diagnosis at all"
"you are not sure about cancer diagnosis"
"there is most likely a tumour, that is of type A"
"malignancy where the histology is not 100 % sure"
"probably cancer of type A"
"the patient has most likely cancer of type A"

  ⌈"it is probably cancer (type A)"
   ⌈"80 - 97 % probability cancer of type A"
 II ⟨ "90 % probability for cancer of type A"
   | "act so that cancer is excluded"
   ⌊"cancer of type A"
from the diagnosticians
   ⌈"it is atypies in A"
 I ⟨ "most likely cancer of type A"
   ⌊"malignant, most likely not adenoca"
 II ⟨ "it should be said in the text that it concerns cancer, but
    ⌊ that the type is difficult to decide"
from language experts:
   ⌈"strange question"
 I ⟨ "P(cancer of type A) > 0.5
   ⌊"should be verified - treat as if..."

The most interesting thing with these answers is that the
doctors might act differently upon the same diagnosis. Many
of them should investigate more. Most of them did not believe
that it was cancer. Some put statistics as interpretations.
But the question is: "Would this diagnosis lead to different
actions? Would some operate? Would some do nothing? Would
some make a new investigation?"

There were very few answers from the diagnosticians. I think
that this depends on the fact that it is their own expressions that are shown and that not everybody uses so many
different expressions. They could not really recognize themselves. From the doctors point of view all these expressions
could appear. My hypothesis is that they hesitate to judge
themselves when they see that there could be so many ways of
expressing something that might be different or might be the
same.

My hypothesis is that the answers from the doctors became
rather different depending on the context of the question.

When the interpretation was to be made in this way:

I "As a clinical doctor how would you interpret a diagnosis like

   ´Most likely cancer of type A´

   ´Cancer, most likely cancer of type A´?"

or in this way:

II "If you were a clinical doctor how would you interpret a diagnosis like

   ´Most likely cancer of type A´

   ´Possibly cancer of type A´

   ´Probably cancer of type A´?"

As answers to the last question came the statistics and definite statements that it was cancer. Question number I gave more loose and uncertain answers.

Worth noting are answers from the doctors such as "more investigation is needed",or "I would have operated in either case" when asking question number II. The doctors say that they would act differently, but these are answers on paper that I have seen; not real actions.

Also, there are few interpretations from the language experts. For them I think it is even worse to put oneself in a clinical doctor´s position to judge or to interpret or to say what they should have done if...

These results are of a very severe nature and should lead to some moves when using a computerized system to its full extent, or to some serious thought before doing so.

5.6 The code "567" - its meanings in the same information system

In a hospital data system I have studied, the code 567 signifies Abracadabra-ill according to an originally objectified pattern, planned by an experienced person in an international list of diagnoses. Abracadabra-ill stands for a diagnosis. 567 should mean exactly the same. There are 300 cases of 567s in one year's records stored in the data system. These 300 diagnoses I have traced back to the original hand and type-written papers in natural work-related language. In these documents the same thing should be said because of the code, but the same diagnosis is not always written. Many variations exist.

Abra-ill, Cadabra-ill, Dabra-ill are some, that is 567 in-cludes more than reality. Mumbo-jumbo + Abracadabra may exist, i.e. one code instead of two. Jumbracadabra shows that 567 embraces too little. Moreover, there is just Mumbo-jumbo, i.e. the wrong code. When I look at the variants that have appeared at least once, there were the following phenomena and their meanings:
- The same person has 567 for quite different diagnoses
- Different people have 567 for quite different diagnoses
- The same person has 567 for overlapping diagnoses
- Different people have 567 for overlapping diagnoses
- The 567 exists when it should have been the 567 + one more code (very common)
- The 567 stands for correct diagnosis, but somewhat more or somewhat aside
- The 567 stands for almost the correct diagnosis, but some is missing
- The 567 was not in natural language BUT JUST IN "567" in the original document

What has been done is that other or additional illnesses "Abracadabra-ill" in the data system has been assigned the code "567", i.e. the code has been applied outside of its formal range of application.

Some secretaries, feeding the data system with diagnoses,

pointed out that they discover these ´faults´ daily. That
such badly coded material has slipped through the system is,
according to the secretaries and others, due to the lack of
medical secretary education. "When the data system was designed the main belief was that it was enough to be a good data
operator in order to be a good data feeder", one physician
told me.

Quality control of measurement is also important and a lot of
this is treated in statistics. Its relevance for information
systems has been discussed and stressed by Kristo Ivanov(1972).

Either we must aim at <u>one</u> denotation with one meaning or we
accept connotations and permit several meanings in multivalent descriptions. A rather context-dependent philosophy has
to replace the existing atomistic view when building data
bases. Moreover, well-trained staff and better control are
needed or the responsibility for the data feeding should be
a matter for the diagnostician.

The personnel are now discussing some improvement concerning
the code system, the reference document and also the data
system.

5.7 Opinons about computers, work and language

In a working group in a department, the members were asked to
fill in five diagrams about different concepts re their own
work. This method emanates from Osgood (Osgood, et al 1957) and
how I use it is described in section 4.7. See also appendix E.

One of the diagrams concerns the "computer display language".
I asked them to associate spontaneously with "computer display language", something between the following pair of evaluating and action-related adjectives:

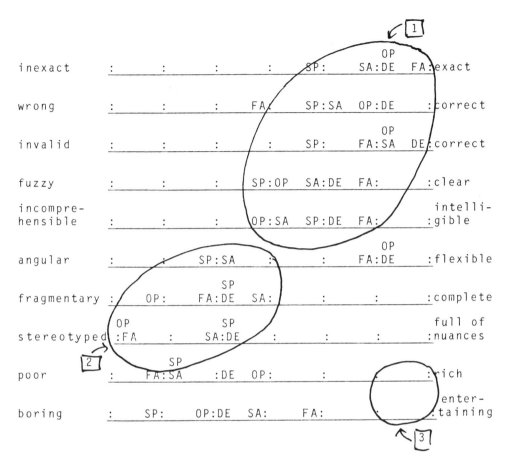

Figure 5.6: Opinions about "computer display language"

The pairs of adjectives above were arranged in another way
when the investigation was made. All the ´positive´ values
were not on the same side as now, when I need to show results
in a more lucid way. The results collected from the 20 people
(of 28 in all; 5 were abscent and 3 did not answer) are marked as follows:

SP   typical value from the sales personnel, three people,
        who use computer based results indirectly

OP   typical value from the order personnel, six people

who take care of the orders from customers

FA   typical value from the four forwarding agents, who
tell the assistants what to do

SA   typical value from the five shipping assistants, who
are face-to-display workers

DE   typical value from the two data experts, who handle the
computer system and the statistics

There were no surprising results from this study. The users
of this data system agreed on the fact that their "computer
display language" is mainly "exact, clear, correct and intel-
ligible" [1] but is also "fragmentary and stereotyped" [2] .
It is neither "rich" nor "entertaining" [3] .

Four similar studies have been made within the same group,
about "computer-based decision bases"
     "computer"
     "your professional knowledge"
     "your job".
The results, comprised in the same kind of diagrams, are
presented in the appendix D on pages D7-D10 in Swedish and on
pages D17-D20 in English. The interpretations by me are the
following:

The group of people handling exports found their computerized
decision bases to be very "useful, interesting and important"
[4] . They really trusted the material mediated by the computer system [5] , and they found it "objective" if they be-
longed to the ordinary users, but as data experts the decision bases in question were rather "subjective", [6] . The
extreme groups - the shipping assistants and the sales personnel - did not find the material as engaging as the middle
group people, who atually worked out the material, [7] .

The "computer" is an "important, indispensable, wellknown, comprehensible and reliable" [8] , machine which is rather "foolish and expensive" [10] . Maybe this is due to the fact that the group was, from my point of view, exactly the right size and that the computer was placed in the same premises, where they worked. They could both see and hear it. The computer was a machine of their own and they had to pay for it out of their own budget. For most of the group, the computer also was fast and faci-litated their work, [9] . However, the shipping assistants found it rather tiring. They fed it with data most of the time.

The opinions on whether computerization has altered their professional knowledge or not, were extremely different. In the cases of alterations quite new jobs were created and people became data feeders and computer maintainers. Almost everyone thought that their professional knowledge had got a positive contribution through computerization both regarding activity [11] , and the contents [12] . The work seemed to be "important and responsible" [13] , and "rich and entertaining" [14] . There seemed to be no conflict between freedom and security. Their work was "both free and safe" and "both creative and formal" [15] - a surprising result. It was due to different definitions of what was meant to be free and safe. The shipping people saw it as a matter of ´to be free´ in work demands first ´to be safe´ in work. From the beginning I looked upon them as competing phenomena. Finally, in general, their work was not especially heavy, [16] .

Looking upon the results as a whole for these people, it can be seen that they would not be happy to lose their computerized system. Even if they do not love their data system, they trust it and feel secure of using it. Maybe they have got so used to it that they do not want to lose it or exchange it because that would disturb the routines. In spite of

this - as a result of my visit - many of the people expressed
enthusiastically that "the system has to be altered; it is
possible to do a lot more" and as an example of the other
extreme, resignedly, that "I could do nothing about the machine". Their use of and the utility of the computerized
information system was focussed upon through my investigation
and there were several discussions on if and how to improve
the system could be improved and some people also questioned
computerization as such.

Summary

In everday life, there are essential phenomena to pay attention to when using and devoping information systems. Tacit
knowledge and learning by experience is one of the main
messages of this chapter, which also takes into account the
sediment of history in the organisations as being difficult
to handle. In my empirical research, I have also studied the
association phenomenon. Some investigations - on the importance of strengthening and weakening words, on the coding of
diagnoses and on people´s opinions of work, language and
computers - and their results, have been presented here (with
the appendices). Studies with the help of Osgood´s semantical
differential are worth repeating in other work groups. They
are soft and well-organized; they are sufficiently anonymous
and not too time-demanding. They could serve as triggers in
order to intervene.

Note

1) The words ´prefix´ and ´suffix´ are not corretly used,
but here they will serve as the analogous meanings they
signify, respectively.

6 Suggested Techniques for Practical Use

6.1 Requirements for support tools for the users

I have suggested earlier some (there are more) kinds of problems concerning information and information systems that are
not easily solved with the techniques of today. A reminder of
them looks like:
- tacit knowledge remains tacit but ´is actually there´
- combination of intuition, logic and experience is necessary
for most problem solving
- sediment may constrain developement and use
- behind an expression there may be several meanings
- associations are difficult to gather
- strengthening and weakening words can be very important
- codes are used instead of normal language

A great deal of research is needed to tackle these ´problems´
from several aspects. Some parts of the problems should
certainly never be ´solved´ but there are ways to go further
with some of them. For instance more awareness is needed of
what systems contain and how systems constrain. I am talking
about information systems in use and information systems that
are going to be used by a person or a group of people in
their daily work.

It is possible to make efforts by letting people apply their
experience of a system, in order to improve its quality. To
do so, it must be possible for the user to develop the system
´in the small´ while using it. In the users´ work as a whole,
we also have to include their tangible and non-tangible
experience and their intuition, whatever this is or might be
defined as. For a thorough presentation of the concept of
´intuition´ see Bastick (1982).

In order to let the users see and share their experiences, their explanations and their intentions, if this is wanted, and in order to facilitate somewhat the combination of intuition and systematics, I will try to develop some tools, an ´augmented thesaurus´ and a ´keep-track-of routine´. In sections 6.4 and 6.5 I will give some hints about the outlines for the two tools.

Several problems are very close to each other and have been discussed by many researchers in different disciplines. (For instance by Eco 1971, Winograd 1973, Rommetveit 1974, Watzlawick et al 1974, Langefors & Sundgren 1975, Lindholm 1979, Codd 1979 and Nissen 1984)

6.2 Decentralized team working parts as served units

It is also important to look into the organization of the work. In order to get good support from a system, the working units should not be too large. Centrally controlled data systems are probably not good foundations for the tools, that I am suggesting to aid in daily work. Also, it is not easy to gain insight into the contents of an information system and its contraints, if the system is too large, too abstract and too remote.

Ideal situations would be work situations with small information systems supporting a working team, which has the possibility of making its own current systems development, parallel to their use. My hypothesis is that it is possible to establish a movement towards more contextual understanding in a decentralized environment with the help of augmented thesauri.

Moreover, another hypothesis is that the thesauri become more realistic in size and extension when they are based on homogeneous linguistic systems for a group, relative to particular situations of use.

6.3 Some technical constructions to improve information systems

In my opinion, an information system should not just contain a data base and some tools for putting in data and retrieving data after 100 % standardized rules stating a designer's opinion of the users' information needs. At least it must be possible to supplement such a one-dimensional catalogue of the data base with an analytical tool and also with a dialectical tool.

When using a data system I suggest that the analytical tool is a keep-track-of routine, which I will describe further in section 6.5.

I suggest that the dialectical tool is an augmented thesaurus, that will be characterized in section 6.4 below.

These three parts - the data base, the augmented thesaurus, the keep-track-of routine - will supplement each other. The catalogue, i.e. the data base schemas, has one dimension and is an inflexible, closed system. It is a sediment, already built and used, rather ineffectively sometimes (see section 5.3), in the organization. It is already known by the users. Anyhow, the data base is the 'new' designers' first building stone. The second one is an augmented thesaurus with several dimensions. It is a flexible and open part with dialectical features. The third stone is the analytical tool with the question: "Who is doing what in a topological structure?" The latter is partly open and is optional.

These ideas are influenced to some extent by Wallin (1980).
He has written about the cata-, ana- and dia-phases in different contexts and I now present a new kind of context in
which these three phases may be applicable. This could also
be seen as evolutionary in time with the catalogue, the data
base, with one dimension as a starting point. Then follows
the dialectic tool, the augmented thesaurus, and lastly the
optional analytical instrument, the keep-track-of routine.

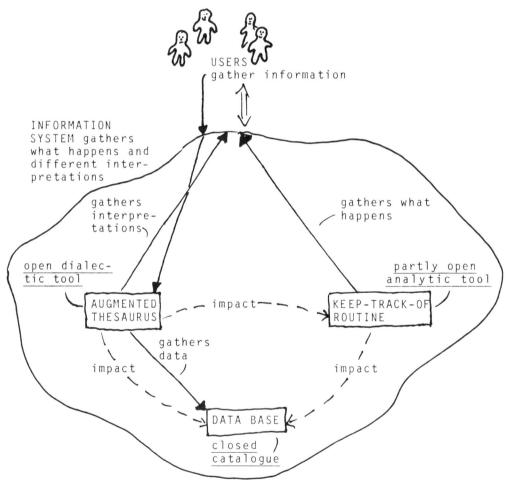

Figure 6.1: The features of a better information system

116

6.4 Augmented thesaurus

6.4.1 Multi-contextual descriptions

An augmented thesaurus can roughly be defined as a Swedish-Swedish (English-English) dictionary with explanations of an expression in contexts, in the event of an action or an intention, in a certain individual´s or group´s perspective. Thus, besides some usual meanings, synonyms and homonymes, it has been extended to include also contextual significations. (Sandström 1981)

An augmented thesaurus should also function as an input quality control concerning the structure and contents, permitted by the user.

The intention is that the multivalent descriptions shall permit several people to interpret an expression. Human beings should be permitted to have different opinions even in a computerized environment. We should be able to build systems to be used by several people or systems that could be used at different times or in different environments without losing the personal touch or shades of meaning to te extent that we are doing today. Not only an augmented thesaurus is needed for this, but also a way to identify who in the first place introduced every elementary or similar message. Even the sender must be traceable so the subjectively differentiated contexts of interpretations can be applied by new/other users. The input control should see to this appliance when securing that input data is recorded with it.

Examples from everyday life confirm that words and sentences, i.e. messages, could have lots of meanings. A word for instance can be explained from the structure, of which it is a part and from the structures it includes. Different kinds of wholes could be imagined or created. A message can be a part

in a description of a work situation. A person's intention
with an expression could also contain the basis for a pragmatic meaning.

An augmented thesaurus may contribute to caution and effectiveness when taking into account the different expressions
and the different interpretations of the phenomena. Elements
of formalism are still there, but they may not feel so one-
sidedly complete and be so devastating.

An augmented thesaurus should be seen as a user's tool that
* facilitates searching for relevant data
* allows systems development 'in the small'
* guides inputs to data systems.

The latter statement concerns control by the thesaurus regarding the structure, the users' permission and optional desires.

Multi-contextual description must be allowed in order to gain
a more flexible system, a more open data system.

6.4.2 To update while utilizing

I propose updating the material supporting a better interpretation of other users' interpretation/application of a fra-
ming schema. This should be done while utilizing the information system, and implies an open system and my intention is
that an augmented thesaurus will function as an opener to the
closed data base in the following sense. The augmented thesaurus is a translator between different people's interpretations of the meanings of expressions. It is a link between
several dimensions. It is a dialectic approach. The users of
the data system in a natural working unit are the bases for
this approach.

An augmented thesaurus such as the one I indicated above,

could be considered as a dictionary with several meanings of an expression, then, now and later on, by several human beings. These human beings are meant to have an impact on the data base in a way that makes their system function as an open system. This system can be changed while using it, because the human being himself is able to put his own expression with his own interpretation into the data system. The data system becomes open through the augmented thesaurus, that allows the human being to introduce and document his interpretation and let another person know that he has done so. But there are difficulties when allowing different interpretations. Statistical comparisons over time are made difficult by such permissions. Other users will also have to be notified that a change has been made or they will not look for a new explanation.

This approach is a possibility for breaking up the traditional way of working with data systems. But this is not the only one. There is also a need for systems´ declarations and for emancipation among the users of data systems. These are less trivial matters that require supplementary research within information science and other disciplines. However, I am discussing this need to some extent, in the last chapter of this report to show that it should not be excluded.

6.4.3 Outlines of multi-contextual descriptions

Parts of these outlines are based principally on Lindholm (1979) and his opinion of ´meaning´. He states that meaning is of something, for somebody, within a context. A phenomenon has - through a perspective within a context - a meaning for a person. Translated and interpreted I have for my purposes re-drawn his figure (ibid p 151) as follows:

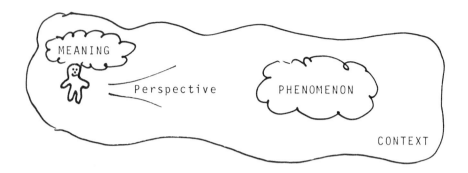

Figure 6.2: The individual meaning of a phenomenon

Earlier in this report I spoke of sociolects (see chapter 2.4). Some of them were on an individual basis and I think it is important to be able to work on the individual level sometimes. On these occasions there could be personal features involved when representating phenomena, even when using a computer in one´s work.

However, people do not always work alone, but rather in groups, ideally in real teamwork groups. Even if they do not have exactly the same perspective on the phenomenon, it might be useful to speak of family language or jargon language at their jobs. The people in the group probably have that much in common that they can agree to use the same expressions in the same way to a great extent, if they not are already doing so.

I will now put the ´individual meaning´ into a wider structure, which enables several ´meanings´ of a ´phenomenon´ to be represented:

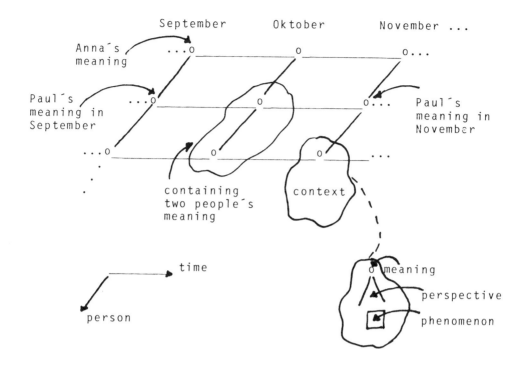

Figure 6.3: The principal structure of multi-contextual de-
            scriptions

The ´person´ is the one defining the source of the message,
usually the sender of the message. The receiver of the message does not have the same authority if the sender and the
receiver are not communicating at the same time.

To represent a person as a receiver/sender or as something
else may be done as follows
    person (Paul, receiver)   person (doctor D, receiver)
    person (Anna, sender)   person (assistant A, sender)
when describing and
    person (Paul, receives)   person (doctor D, receives)
    person (Anna, sends)   person (assistant A, sends)
when communicating.

An "expression" could be a normal sentence or a sign. When
nothing else is said, an "expression" could be agreed to be
the same as a message with "object", "property", "property
value", "quality mark" and "measuring time" (cf Langefors
1966 & Ivanov 1972). It can, however, be seen as an intention
without an intender, a kind of objectified message. As soon
as a real person says something, it may be possible to tell
this and the time the message is sent and to choose other
representation structures when informing each other. The
structure might be chosen individually or chosen in mutual
agreement. It could also be a structure, where one can show
intentions behind the message or a structure, which is likely
to indicate some of the perspectives of the sender.

We need to represent several types of shapes, such as intentions, explanations, perspectives and/or surroundings, together with the sign or the sentence and the quality of the
contents in several instances. It might also be important to
know the time when the message is received. See below (6.4.4
- 6.4.6)

The purpose of the message creating process is to choose
object and properties according to a criterion of one's own.
The question is: what is most important among the properties
(the connotations), for somebody on a specific occasion? It
should be denoting and it must not always be the same. The
possibility of chosing between the most common structure or
the agreed structure and an optional statement could be based
upon:

```
STRUCTURE        ->    structure(BOUND   FREE)
BOUND            ->    bound(MESSAGE   MESSAGE-PART)
MESSAGE          ->    message(<OBJECT> <PROPERTIES>)
PROPERTIES       ->    PROPERTY  , PROPERTY
MESSAGE-PART     ->    message-part(OBJECT   PROPERTY)
FREE             ->    free(SENTENCE   WORD   SIGN)
```

```
SENTENCE            ->    sentence("S")
WORD                ->    word("W")
SIGN                ->    sign("&")
```

```
where  ->    means    defines as
             means    or
             means    is to be repeated 0 or several times
```

in a syntax examplified with

```
  STRUCTURE:  structure(bound(message(<paul> <patient,sick>)))
  MESSAGE:    message(<paul> <patient, sick>)
  SENTENCE:   sentence("patient Paul is sick")
  WORD:       word("Hallo!")
  SIGN:       sign("£")
```

The structure could be bound or free, relative to some pre-
established norms. The structure shown above is just an
example, according to Backus-Naur Form (Goldschlager & Lister
1982 pp. 179-182), with two forms, a message form and a sentence form as I defined them. It is possible to form any
structure as long as formal grammar is retained.

The ´time´ is very important in at least two ways, the time
(1) when defining - when sending or receiving - the message
and the time (2) during which the message content is valid:

```
(1)     person(anna, receives("11 Oct 1984", MESSAGES)
(2)     message(<paul> <patient, sick, from84-10-09>)
(2)     message(<peter> <patient, sick, 84-10-01--84-10-08>)
```

6.4.4 To represent intentional expressions

In order to represent intentions, I have adopted an idea
presented by Dennett (1983). His first point about intentio-
nality is

  "that we can rely on a marked set of idioms to have this
  special feature of being sensitive to the means of referen-

ce used in the clauses they introduce. The most familiar
such idioms are "believes", that", "knows that", "expects
(that)", "wants (it to be the case that)", "recognizes
(that)", "understands (that)".
His second point is that
   "the use of intentional idioms carries a presupposition or
   assumption of rationality in the creature or system to
   which the intentional states are attributed." (ibid. p.345)

There could be different orders of intentional sentences (cf.
Nissen 1984a). Such a creature of system is capable of
handling:

intentional order of sentence	examples
Zero-order	Patient P is sick
First-order	Doctor D believes that Patient P is sick
Second-order	Doctor D believes that Assistant A knows that Patient P is sick
Third-order	Doctor D understands that Assistant A wants him to believe that Patient P is sick
Fourth-order	Doctor D believes that Assistant A wants him(D) to think that he(A) knows that Patient P is sick

and so on, in principle for ever, but there is an upper limit
to how much it is reasonable to manage even with the help of
a computer.

The sentences of different intentional order might be written
as follows, more formally, with the help of parentheses as
structuring symbols. (See for instance Clocksin & Mellish
1981)

        (P is sick)
        believes(D, P is sick)
        believes(D, knows(A, P is sick))

```
        understands(D, wants(A, believes(D, P is sick)))
        believes(D, wants(A, thinks(D, knows(A, P is sick)))))
```
These are easy to translate into a logic programming language
and can then easily be handled by a computer.

In any genuine communication between people, there are at
least third-order intentional sentences involved and this can
be reflected also in computerized information systems. In
some way we have to involve the sender and the receiver
together with their intentions, visibly, even if they are not
physically present.

6.4.5 To represent perspectives behind expressions

In order to make explicit the perspective in which a work
related phenomenon is presented, I have at least to take into
account causes, purposes and effects. Thus, there must exist
possibilities to represent messages intentionally and pre-
dictably in an augmented thesaurus. These aims stand for a
person's desire to display what he really means, i.e. to
explain what has happened or to show his will or to predict
an effect. An explanation points backwards to the causes. A
prediction points forwards to a plausible effect. An intention influences forwards in a will. I would like to present
such views as explicitly as possible. These different perspectives can be represented in a similar way:

```
            intention ---> message
        explanation <--- message
            message ---> prediction
            message ---> action
```

The three perspectives can then easily be represented in the
same logical expressions as the intention levels above. These
expressions are examples only to indicate a kind of formalism
to go further within the area. The following examples will
probably illustrate this:

```
      believes(D, P is sick) -> (P is sick)
                 diagnosis <- (P is sick)
            (P is sick) -> (operation on P tomorrow)
(operation tomorrow 10 a.m.) -> to cure P I will operate on
                         his heart ..
```

The expressions could be interpreted :
    If doctor D believes that P is sick then P is sick.
    P is sick according to the diagnosis or according to
      doctor E who assigned the diagnosis.
    P is sick and an operation will probably take place.
    As the plan is to operate on P tomorrow at 10 I then do so.

6.4.6 To represent surroundings of expressions

When (1966) Langefors presented the ´message concept´ it also
contained the ´system´ around the object, for which the
´properties´ were to be measured. In order to save computer
memory, he later on (1970) suggested a concept of ´concepts´
as a structure for the properties in the messages. These two
ways of describing environments have not been developed to
any great extent, in order to achieve this efficiency or in
order to achieve the purposes I have suggested.

These two good ideas may be better exploited now when we need
not think of computer memory saving. Rather, there is a lot
to gain in effectiveness through better understanding, when
we more frequently and explicitly see the meaning of, for instance, the ´property´ "price" as a description of how setting prices is done. We must also have rules for when we must
not omit the description of ´system´ in the messages.

In order to see the surroundings, where we find the messages
and the piece of work in question, and to shape representa-
tions for them, we have to know the jargon language around
the work within the team. The single user of an information

system has his own language and there will be no problem as long as he does not change his mind and starts forgetting his own previous meanings, not explicitly documented or otherwise shown. It is, however, extremely unusual to have just one user in a particular job, as both sender and receiver of the mediated information. Thus, we normally have more than one user. As soon as there are several users we have the problem of how to gather and document the surroundings for the whole team in order to improve data base praxis of today. The surroundings described belong, with the descriptions of perspectives, to the context of an expression.

I mean that the context of an expression, when getting a visible text around it, must grow out from the team itself and then be described or be decided by the users beforehand and then be described to avoid severe misunderstandings.

The larger the group, the more has normally to be decided beforehand. We must introduce rules and descriptions of examples when learning how to use the system. We need this for new employees in the actual team and for new users outside the team. Three different kinds of users are now in question:
- the individual person with his own work habit with the information system
- the indivuduals of the group with a common language base, well acquainted with the agreed structure and the user rules
- people outside the group

Depending on who the user is, different kinds of descriptions are important. These descriptions have to cover the user rules, the jargon language and should be given in plain language, using examples. Learning by examples, fetched for instance in a diary of earlier uses, could then be of interest. Such earlier learning, as own experience of usage might be documented and might funtion as a substitute for a manual. (cf. Järvinen 1983)

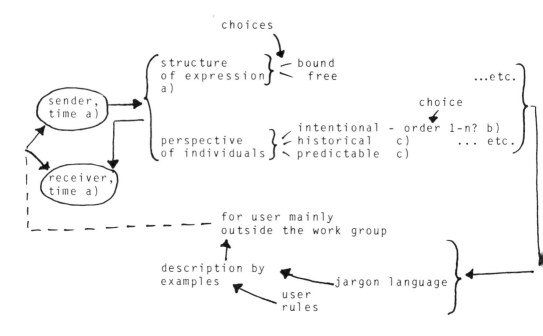

a) see section 6.4.3 for examples
b) see "   6.4.4 "   "
c) see "   6.4.5 "   "

Figure 6.4: Overview of the logical representation structure
            for multi-contextual descriptions

6.5 Keep-track-of routine

In connection with discussions about the development of a
retrieval system within an economic activity of an enterprise, I direct some of the users and some of the developers
towards the idea of a keep-track-of routine as an optional
aid. This should mainly keep track of the activity of an
individual and a group, when working at a data terminal with
their new retrieval system. The routine will also take care
of how a certain problem, a particular task or case, or a set
of similar tasks or cases have been handled. Moreover, it
should be possible to know whether something is e.g. a speci-

fic recorded mistake about a diagnosis that has been discovered through a retrieval process, whether it has been corrected or not, and if so to what extent this has influenced
other parts referred to.

The contents of a data base will be changed in use. This
change is subjective from the particular user's point of
view. It could be used further as a possible objective description in an optional way for this user or a group of
users.

Moreover, one person can use the data base more frequently
than another. One person can do this in a special manner or
in a special field several times. This knowledge in the form
of statistics will be useful later when the same person uses
the base again. Options and statistics in this direction have
been worked out with some success in the Markisett-project
(Glimell 1975).

Thus, a keep-track-of routine is meant to be an easily acces-
sible follow-up for the user in a retrieval situation. The
aim of the routine is to make improved activities possible. I
believe that the routine will:
- support the individual or the group in daily work
- on average need less time for handling a task
- raise the chance of getting correct decision bases.
The routine is also based on the augmented thesaurus, where
the meanings of expressions are of great importance. It
should function upon the users' demands.

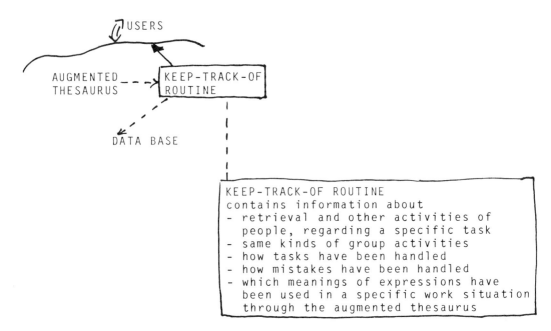

Figure 6.4: The keep-track-of routine

The augmented thesaurus gathers the interpretations of the users' expressions and the keep-track-of routine gathers what happens in the course of the work, but the augmented thesaurus naturally has an impact on the keep-track-of routine. This routine is partly open and unbiased and by that I mean that it absorbs and almost one-sidedly requires, what happens through uncoloured glass. The colour, i.e. the perspective, comes from the thesaurus with its expressions in contexts, perspectives and intentions for each individual. Both the tools I suggest have an impact on the content and structure of the data base. (See also figure 6.1)

If we have the possibility of describing phenomena in several contexts from different perspectives, we may also keep track of who has done what and how and within where. We may be better off knowing what we are talking about and also knowing which version of interpretation is valid and whose expressions are being used. To what extent is a mistake, a fault, corrected throughout an information system? How was a specific task handled in a specific situation in a specific section of a department? These are questions that I intend to make answerable by means of a keep-track-of routine.

´Within where´ might be a dated short description of the situation, of the job as such. Who has done what and how, might be described as "I am doing this task for my own work (or for the group work) This task, mistake/fault has been treated so far in this way, for this account, in that department." in positive terms. It could also be said negatively for example: "This mistake has not been corrected within such-and-such a task." If the work related expressions in the texts are expressed in an unusual or agreed upon meaning this should also be clarified.

Such a routine is also based on logical structuring, however, and therefore it becomes a programmed tool with limitations, which must be clarified for the users. There are always upper limits for flexibility, and users must be aware of these constraints in a computerized information system.

6.6 Some usable programs

Good programs with similar features as described earlier in this chapter, have already been made by some researchers.

The natural language is used as a basis by Winograd in his SHRDLU (Winograd 1972), discussed and very well described also in Boden (1981). TEIRESIAS (Davis 1976) is another system, the point of which is to ´listen´ in order to aid users in augmenting and modifying their expert system. The

program has been utilized within the medical field. A third
system worth mentioning, is the HACKER, build by Sussman
(1973). The main feature of it is ´learning by doing´. Doyle
(1980 has used HACKER for formalization of the concepts of
goal and intention.

Summary

In order to let the users share their experiences, even when
using a computerized information system, I suggest that a
data base should be supplemented with an augmented thesaurus
and a keep-track-of routine. The properties of these two
tools have been described as prerequisites and presuppositions, based upon the wishes of the end-users. The augmented
thesaurus is supposed to be an open dialectic tool for the
users, while the keep-track-of routine is a partly open
analytical tool for the users. The most important features of
this thesaurus are the continous updating and the multi-
contextual descriptions. The most important feature of this
keep-track-of routine is the parallel handling of activities,
tasks, mistakes and meanings.

7 Summarizing Arguments

7.1 Discoveries

Hitherto I have found the following:

Many administrative computerized information systems in use, envisage a benefit- and cost-relation that is clearly inferior to what it should be. Benefits and costs also have to include intrinsic and intangible entities.

The utility of most of the administration systems depends on how the users´ actions are influenced by the information they get, or can themselves obtain from the systems. This influence is developed while the systems are being used.

How an end-user will act upon a piece of information depends largely on how they interpret it. A correct interpretation is important even among those who furnish a computerized system with information. There are needs for contexual descriptions of work related phenomena.

Until now, such questions of interpretation might have been treated in connection with systems specifications. The interpretation then standardized, has become the one that is presupposed everybody will use as a matter of course. This presupposition will not always exist in practical life.

Therefore, a systems design needs to conceive computer-based tools, which makes it easier for the end-user to interpret correctly, expressions mediated by the computerized iniormation system and to make better use of the possible basis for the more purposeful actions that they have in a data base.

7.2 Continuous Systems development ´in the small´

The basic idea behind the whole research work, has been to
make it possible for the user to develop the information
system when new needs appear. There need not always be a lot
of analyzing work and financial investment to motivate a
necessary change. The idea is to let users acquire knowledge
and self-confidence to be able to more and more judge by
themselves which kind of computer information system really
supported them in their work and which did not. The increased
self-confidence should make them secure enough to convey
their judgements both to their bosses and to any experts who
care to listen. It is not at all impossible to let the users
themselves take responsibility for these kinds of changes.
They know best whether changes are needed or not. This must
not be a business for a system designer or a machine supplier
to the same extent as it has been before. Personnel outside
the work situation must be involved only when they are influenced by it or have a special interest in it. Systems
development ´in the small´ costs little effort when carried
out and much self-esteem is gained, through ´knowing how´ and
when (Ryle 1949) in work as a whole, and in adequate information support, through making alterations if and when needed.

When speaking of the responsibility above, I would like to
refer to Nurminen who argues that man should be responsible
for both job and information. Responsibility does not appear
only as accountability:

"Responsibility means being responsible. Beyond the usual
meaning related with accountability we will try to find
another connotation from the root "respond". In the context of information systems, the receiver is able to
respond to a message, if he can use it correctly at his
work. This naturally requires a genuine understanding of
the message, not only stimulus-response type of behavior.
So we understand that a responsible user of information

understands the pragmatic meaning... . It will be argued
that this pragmatic understanding creates a good prere-
quisite for accountability." (Nurminen 1982 p. 6.4)

It is also very important to care about the employee resources within an enterprise. The employees must have varying
work and be trusted to handle their own information systems.
They are also the people who best know their own information
requirements and how they should be presented and it is a
waste of resources not to take advantage of their knowledge
when they utilize the information system. It may also be possible to get rid of most of the unnecessary sediment that
nobody normally questions in daily work. The men do not feel
responsible or they do not even see it, because they do not
really understand.

In principal however, there are no clearly defined obstacles
for greater investment of people, users and experts, and
time, in systems development initiated by new technology, or
radical changes in the work and organization, due to the fact
that the old computer is ready for the scrap-heap.

7.3 A well-balanced decentralization of the information resources

To gather the end-users´ ideas of improvements in their information system is important. It is also essential that the
end-users themselves execute the ideas immediately in the
existing work situations. The situation I speak of is rather
clearly outlined work with small computerized information
systems as support for the individuals. They could also be
teamwork. The group of people should have the possibilities
to take in the consequences of realizing their ideas and
their solutions to their own problems, regarding the information they need.

I have made some outlines for an augmented thesaurus and a
keep-track-of routine as user support tools.These tools will
have to be used as supplements to each other and to the
data base, of course. A general sketch of this co-operation
is made and further empirical work is going on to test and
develop the tools for the end-users and also with their help
in an administration department of a Swedish company.

After having accumulated the problems from reality and consulted some researchers, I have good reasons to believe that
it is an excellent idea to use together an augmented thesaurus, a keep-track-of routine and so-called service explanations (cf Nissen 1981) of information systems for specific
use. Each information system will be seen as a particular one
and be defined as a result of well-balanced decentralization.

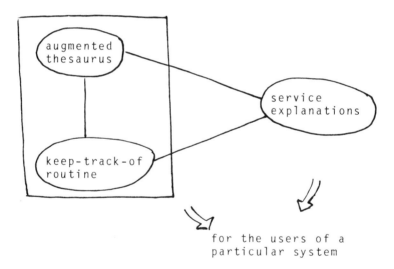

for the users of a
particular system

Figure 7.1: Foundation stones for better information systems

A qualitative declaration of systems is needed, with information about what services you can get from the system. (Nissen
1981 p. 8) Requirement specifications in systems´ analyses
are often written on the conditions of the designers and in
their particular language, but knowledge that appears during

the specific work must be presented in the users´ language in
service explanations, in the augmented thesaurus and for
further systems development.

Sometimes, in the case of unstructured or soft problems, the
´change´ envisaged is the creation and implementation of a
problem (cf Checkland 1981). Here it might be an alternative,
worth testing, to specify and implement the two system parts
"augmented thesaurus" and "keep-track-of routine" and describe their possibilities and constraints in service explanations.

7.4 Further research regarding the use of information systems

Research within the realm of "use of information systems" is
urgent and there is a great deal of work left undone for further
efforts. My proposal is limited to containing research on the
use of information, mediated by data systems for a specific
task. I think my work is promising enough to investigate
further, within the social and technological fields of the
information and computer sciences, regarding the interpretation
of formalized or computerized information and also the way in
which this information can be acted upon.

We need more empirical material from different work fields re
the understanding and acting upon information supported by
data systems.

An interest in emancipation is also important and belief in
the intervening approach when doing such research. To integ-
rate quantitave and qualitative methods in this work must be
tested in order to progress. Also methods for measuring other
kinds of values than economic ones, must be worked out.

To declare what a system really is capable of, is one of the most important matters to go forward with. An investigation of how this is done at present maybe a starting point.

Technicians should collect requirements based on practical needs, rather than invest efforts in advertising a tool for which they are not sure that there is a need. The augmented thesaurus and the keep-track-of routine are now to be programmed and tested and may serve as examples of requirements from practical life, from groups of individuals who are using computer-based information systems.

So far, this has been expressed in a more general way. For more concrete further research within Lund I propose

- a few more empirical investigations concerning interpretation and action based upon information from computerized systems and concerning opinions of work, language and computers

- detailed performance and implementation, together with the end-users in some organizations, of augmented thesauri and keep-track-routines, for test and evaluation by the end-users

- to find out how information systems are described in handbooks and in internal education, how these are understood and used in some organizations

- to investigate the desires of end-users and the tecnical possibilities for utilizing pictures, grafics, words and calculations.

From these proposals, I expect results that show the importance of taking into account interpretation and action in connection with the use and the development of information systems, and that give the possibilities for a continuous increase in quality, regarding the contents and the use of

computerized information systems. Such research will hopefully contribute to the theory of future development and use of
information system.

The practical value of the research, that I already have
done or that I propose, may be of direct benefit both

* to users of information systems, through new features of
quality, and

* to designers of information systems, through the possibilities of conceiving qualitatively, quite new functions in
administrative systems.

Appendices

APPENDIX A in Swedish (English translation on pages A3-A4)

Gunhild Sandström   mars 1984
Informationsbehandling-ADB
Lunds Universitet

ENKÄT OM ANVÄNDNING AV BEGREPP
EXEMPEL FRÅN DATASYSTEMET "ZZZ" PÅ AVDELNINGARNA "bbb" och "ccc"

Förklara för en utomstående nedanstående begrepp med dina egna helt vanliga
ord. Ange dels hur du normalt skulle definiera begreppet om en utomstående
skulle fråga: "Vad betyder <BEGREPPET>?" och dels i vilket sammanhang du
mest använder begreppet. Om du inte begriper ett dugg tala om det. Om du har
haft en innebörd för begreppet som försvunnit för dig, skriv att du glömt bort
den. Var så tydlig du kan. Skriv hellre för mycket än för litet. Använd papper
vid sidan om eller baksidorna av formuläret om det behövs. Det är ingen
kontroll av kunskaper som just du måste ha. Tänk inte för länge. Använd inte
hjälpmedel. Diskutera inte med dina kamrater.

Tack för den hjälp du ger genom dina svar. De kommer att behandlas konfi-
dentiellt.

BEGREPP[a]

'PAPILLÄRT HIDRADENOM'
Definition:

Användning:

'PRIMÄR SPOTTKÖRTELFÖRÄNDRING' [b]

'TROPISK SPRUE'

---
[a] Begreppen började på ny sida i undersökningen.
[b] Alla begrepp har rubrikerna "Definition:" och "Användning:" såsom under
'PAPILLÄRT HIDRADENOM'.

'BIOPSI'

'OSTEOCHONDROMATOS'

'MÅTTLIG ATYPI'

'SANNOLIKT SKIVEPITELCANCER'

'PROVTYP'

'EKTOPI GLIAVÄVNAD'

'SNABBFIX'

'LEUKEMOID REAKTION'

'PROLIFERATION'

'METASTAS ADENOCA'

'SYSTEMSJUKDOM'

'LEIOMYOM EPITELOIDSCELLS'

'IMPRINT'

'GLOMUSTUMÖR'

'ADENOMYOS'

'STILLSAM CELLBILD'

''PAD'-REMISS'

APPENDIX A English translation

Gunhild Sandström   March 1984
Information and Computer Sciences
Lund University, Sweden

QUESTIONNAIRE ON THE USE OF EXPRESSIONS,
EXAMPLE FROM THE SYSTEM "ZZZ" IN THE DEPARTMENTS "bbb" and "ccc"

Explain to the uninitiated the following concepts in the words you usually use.
State how you normally would define the concept if an outsider should ask.
"What does ‹THE CONCEPT› stand for?" as well as in which context you mostly
use the concept. If you do not understand at all, say so. If you have previously
had an interpretation of the concept, which you have forgotten, put that you
cannot remember it. Be as clear as you can. Write rather too much than too
little. Use an extra paper or the back of this formula, if needed. This is not a
cheque on the knowledge that you must have. Do not think too much. Do not use
dictionaries or discuss with your fellow-workers.

Thank you for the help you give.through your answers. They will be treated
confidentially.

CONCEPTS[a]

'PAPILLAR HIDRADENOMA'
Definition:

Use:

'PRIMARY CHANGE IN SALIVARY GLAND'[b]

'TROPICAL SPRUE'

-----

[a] The concepts started on a new page in the investigation.
[b] All the concepts have the headings "Definition" and "Use" as under the
'PAPILAR HIDRADENOMA'.

'BIOPSY'

'OSTEOCHONDROMATOS'

'MODERATE ATYPIA'

'PROBABLE SKIVEPITHELCANCER'

'SAMPLE TYPE'

'EKTOPI GLIA-TISSUE'

'QUICKLY FIXED SAMPLE'

'LEUKEMOID REACTION'

'PROLIFERATION'

'METASTAS ADENOCA'

'SYSTEMS DISEASE'

'LEIOMYOM EPITELOIDSCELLS'

'IMPRINT'

'GLOMUSTUMOR'

'ADENOMYOS'

'MODERATE CELL PICTURE'

''PAD'-REFERENCE'

APPENDIX B in Swedish (English translation on pages B6-B10)

FRÅGEFORMULÄR OCH SVAR RÖRANDE FÖRSTÄRKANDE OCH FÖRSVAGANDE ORD

Formulär I

Gunhild Sandström   oktober 1984
Informationsbehandling-ADB
Lunds Universitet

Hej!

Jag är forskare inom informationsbehandling. Av Arbetarskyddsfonden, Styrelsen för Teknisk Utveckling och Lunds Universitet har jag fått forsknings-medel som bl a nyttjas för att undersöka begrepp och begreppstolkning i samband med bruk av informationssystem på sjukhus.

Jag skulle gärna vilja veta hur du som språkkunnig/kliniker/diagnostisör rangordnar inom var och en av följande två grupper av uttryck:

malignitet kan ej uteslutas   sannolikt cancer
stark misstanke om malignitet   möjligen cancer
malignitet kan ej helt uteslutas   troligen cancer
misstanke om malignitet
viss misstanke om malignitet

Ordna med hjälp av siffrorna 1, 2 osv. Ju högre siffra ju mera sjuk patient. Ingenting hindrar att olika uttryck får samma värde.

Om du vore kliniker hur skulle du tolka diagnossvar som

sannolikt cancer av typ A
möjligen cancer av typ A
troligen cancer av typ A.

Tack för din hjälp. Du får se resultatet. Ditt svar kan du sända mig i bilagt kuvert.

Vänliga hälsningar
Gunhild Sandström

144

Formulär II

Gunhild Sandström   november 1984
Informationsbehandling-ADB
Lunds Universitet

Hej!

Jag är forskare inom informationsbehandling. Av Arbetarskyddsfonden, Styrelsen för Teknisk Utveckling och Lunds Universitet har jag fått forsknings-
medel som bl a nyttjas för att undersöka begrepp och begreppstolkning i
samband med bruk av informationssystem på sjukhus.

Jag skulle gärna vilja veta hur du som diagnostisör/kliniker rangordnar inom
var och en av följande två grupper av uttryck:

malignitet kan ej uteslutas   sannolikt cancer
stark misstanke om malignitet   möjligen cancer
malignitet kan ej helt uteslutas   troligen cancer
misstanke om malignitet
viss misstanke om malignitet

Ordna med hjälp av siffrorna 1, 2 osv. Ju större siffra ju mera sjuk patient.
Ingenting hindrar att olika uttryck får samma värde.

Om/som kliniker hur skulle du i ord tolka diagnossvar som

A. Sannolikt cancer av typ A.
B. Cancer, sannolikt cancer av typ A.
   Svar:

Tack för din hjälp. Du får se resultatet. Ditt svar kan du sända mig i bilagt
kuvert.

Vänliga hälsningar
Gunhild Sandström

Svar

.........FRÅN 15 DIAGNOSTISÖRER..........

på formulär I

rangordningsriktning[a] diagnostext	↑	↑	↑	↑	↑	↑	↑	↑
malignitet kan ej uteslutas	2	2	3	1	2	4	2	2
stark misstanke om malignitet	3	4	5	1	5	5	4	4
malignitet kan ej helt uteslutas	1	1	2	1	1	2	1	1
misstanke om malignitet	2	3	4	1	4	4	3	3
viss misstanke om malignitet	1	1	3	1	3	3	1	1
sannolikt cancer	3	2	2	1	5	2	2	2
möjligen cancer	1	1	1	1	3	1	1	1
troligen cancer	2	2	2	1	5	1	2	2
sannolikt cancer av typ A	3	b)	3	1	5	2	2	2
möjligen cancer av typ A	1	b)	2	1	3	1	1	1
troligen cancer av typ A	2	b)	3	1	5	1	2	2

fortsättning	på formulär I			på formulär II			
rangordningsrikting[a] diagnostext	↑	↑	↑	↑	↑	↑	↓
malignitet kan ej uteslutas	1	2	2	2	1	2	3
stark misstanke om malignitet	3	4	3	4	3	5	1
malignitet kan ej helt uteslutas	1	1	1	1	1	1	4
misstanke om malignitet	2	3	2	3	2	4	2
viss misstanke om malignitet	1	1	1	2	1	3	3
sannolikt cancer	2	4	2	2	3	5	1
möjligen cancer	1	2	1	1	1	3	4
troligen cancer	1	3	2	2	2	5	1
sannolikt cancer av typ A	2	4	b)				
möjligen cancer av typ A	1	2	b)				
troligen cancer av typ A	1	3	b)				

---

[a] ↑ innebär att "högre siffra" (i formulär I) har tolkats som att 2 representerar mera än 1 och ↓ innebär att "högre siffra" har tolkats som att 1 representerar mera än 2.

[b] Tolkning i ord.

Svar

....................FRÅN 18 KLINIKLÄKARE...................
på formulär I   på formulär

rangordningsriktning[a] diagnostext	↑	↓	↑	↓	↑	↑	↓	↑	↑	↑
malignitet kan ej uteslutas	2	4	2	4	2	3	4	1	2	4
stark misstanke om malignitet	3	1	5	1	5	5	1	4	5	5
malignitet kan ej helt uteslutas	2	5	1	5	1	1	5	2	1	1
misstanke om malignitet	3	2	4	2	4	4	2	3	4	3
viss misstanke om malignitet	2	3	3	3	3	2	3	2	3	2
sannolikt cancer	3	1	3	1	3	2	1	2	3	3
möjligen cancer	3	3	1	3	1	1	3	1	1	1
troligen cancer	3	2	2	2	2	2	2	1	2	2
sannolikt cancer av typ A	3	b)	b)	b)	3	b)	1			
möjligen cancer av typ A	3	b)	b)	b)	1	b)	3			
troligen cancer av typ A	3	b)	b)	b)	2	b)	2			

fortsättning rangordningsrikting[a] diagnostext	på formulär II							
	↑	↑	↑	↑	↑	↑	↑	↑
malignitet kan ej uteslutas	5	4	3	2	2	3	2	2
stark misstanke om malignitet	6	5	5	5	3	4	5	6
malignitet kan ej helt uteslutas	4	1	2	1	1	2	1	1
misstanke om malignitet	3	3	4	4	2	2	4	4
viss misstanke om malignitet	1	2	1	3	1	1	3	3
sannolikt cancer	7	8	5	6	3	2	3	7
möjligen cancer	2	6	2	4	1	1	1	5
troligen cancer	6	7	4	5	2	2	2	7

---

a) ↑ innebär att "högre siffra" (i formulär I) har tolkats som att 2 representerar mera än 1 och ↓ innebär att "högre siffra" har tolkats som att 1 representerar mera än 2.
b) Tolkning i ord.

B5

Svar

.................FRÅN 9 SPRÅKFORSKARE................
på formulär I

rangordningsriktning[a] diagnostext	↓	↓	↓	↑	↓	↑	↑ ↑[c]	↓	↑
malignitet kan ej uteslutas	4	3	3	3	3	2	1 2[c]	4	2
stark misstanke om malignitet	1	1	1	5	1	5	2 5	1	5
malignitet kan ej helt uteslutas	5	2	5	1	4	1	1 1	5	1
misstanke om malignitet	2	3	2	4	2	4	2 4	2	4
viss misstanke om malignitet	3	4	3	2	3	3	2 3	3	3
sannolikt cancer	2	1	1	2	1	3	2 3	1	2 3[d]
möjligen cancer	3	2	3	1	2	1	1 1	3	1
troligen cancer	1	1	2	2	1	2	2 2	2	2 2
sannolikt cancer av typ A	–	1	1	b)	b)	3	2 3	1	b)
möjligen cancer av typ A	–	2	3	b)	b)	1	1 1	3	b)
troligen cancer av typ A	–	1	2	b)	b)	2	2 2	2	b)

---

[a] ↑ innebär att "högre siffra" (i formulär I) har tolkats som att 2 representerar mera än 1 och ↓ innebär att "högre siffra" har tolkats som att 1 representerar mera än 2.

[b] Tolkning i ord.

[c] Som patient kolumnen till vänster; som forskare kolumnen till höger.

[d] Som person kolumnen till vänster; som forskare kolumnen till höger.

APPENDIX B English translation

QUESTIONNAIRE AND ANSWERS REGARDING STRENGTHENING AND WEAKENING WORDS

Formula I

Gunhild Sandström   October 1984
Information and Computer Sciences
Lund University, Sweden

Hallo!

I am a researcher in information and computer sciences and my work is financed by The Swedish Work Environment Fund, The National Swedish Board for Technical Development and Lund University. The grant is, among other things, is used to investigate concepts and their interpretations in connection with the use of information systems at your hospital.

I would like to know how you, as a linguist/clinical doctor/diagnostician, rank the following expressions, within each of the two groups:

malignancy cannot be excluded   most likely cancer
strong suspicion of malignancy   possibly cancer
malignancy cannot be entirely excluded   probably cancer
suspicion of malignancy
some suspicion of malignancy

Rank, with the help of the figures 1, 2 etc. The higher figure the more sick.the patient. Nothing prevents different expressions from getting the same value.

If you were a clinical doctor, how would you interpret diagnosis answers such as:

most likely cancer of type A
possibly cancer of type A
probably cancer of type A

Thank you for your help. You may see the result. You can send me your answer in the enclosed envelope.

Yours sincerely
Gunhild Sandström

Formula II

Gunhild Sandström
Information and Computer Sciences
Lund University, Sweden

November 1984

Hallo!

I am a researcher in information and computer sciences and my work is financed by The Swedish Work Environment Fund, The National Swedish Board for Technical Development and Lund University. The grant, among other things, is used to investigate concepts and their interpretations in connection with the use of information systems at your hospital.

I would like to know how you as a linguist/clinical doctor/diagnostician rank the following expressions, within each of the two groups:

malignancy cannot be excluded   most likely cancer
strong suspicion of malignancy   possibly cancer
malignancy cannot be entirely excluded   probably cancer
suspicion of malignancy
some suspicion of malignancy

Rank with the help of the figures 1, 2 etc. The larger figure the more sick the patient. Nothing prevents different expressions from getting the same value.

If/as a clinical doctor, how would you in words interpret diagnosis answers such as.

most likely cancer of type A
cancer, most likely cancer of type A

Thank you for your help. You may see the result. You can send me your answer in the enclosed envelope.

Yours sincerely
Gunhild Sandström

Answers   ....FROM 15 DIAGNOSTICIANS...........

on formula I

ranking direction[a] texts from diagnoses	↑	↑	↑	↑	↑	↑	↑	↑
malignancy cannot be excluded	2	2	3	1	2	4	2	2
strong suspicion of malignancy	3	4	5	1	5	5	4	4
malignancy cannot be entirely excluded	1	1	2	1	1	2	1	1
suspicion of malignancy	2	3	4	1	4	4	3	3
som suspicion of malignancy	1	1	3	1	3	3	1	1
most likely cancer	3	2	2	1	5	2	2	2
possibly cancer	1	1	1	1	3	1	1	1
probably cancer	2	2	2	1	5	1	2	2
most likely cancer of type A	3	b)	3	1	5	2	2	2
possibly cancer of type A	1	b)	2	1	3	1	1	1
probably cancer of type A	2	b)	3	1	5	1	2	2

continuing   in formula I   in formula II

ranking direction[a] texts from diagnoses	↑	↑	↑	↑	↑	↑	↓
malignancy cannot be excluded	1	2	2	2	1	2	3
strong suspicion of malignancy	3	4	3	4	3	5	1
malignancy cannot be entirely excluded	1	1	1	1	1	1	4
suspicion of malignancy	2	3	2	3	2	4	2
some suspicion of malignancy	1	1	1	2	1	3	3
most likely cancer	2	4	2	2	3	5	1
possibly cancer	1	2	1	1	1	3	4
probably cancer	1	3	2	2	2	5	1
most likely cancer of type A	2	4	b)				
possibly cancer of type A	1	2	b)				
probably cancer of type A	1	3	b)				

---

a) ↑ means that "higher figure" (in formula I) has been inteterpreted so that 2 represents more than 1 and ↓ means that "higher figure" has been interpreted so that 1 represents more than 2.

b) Interpretation in words

ANSWERS

ranking direction[a)] texts from diagnoses	on formula I							on formula II		
	↑	↓	↑	↓	↑	↑	↓	↑	↑	↑
malignancy cannot be excluded	2	4	2	4	2	3	4	1	2	4
strong suspicion of malignancy	3	1	5	1	5	5	1	4	5	5
malignancy cannot be entirely excluded	2	5	1	5	1	1	5	2	1	1
suspicion of malignancy	3	2	4	2	4	4	2	3	4	3
some suspicion of malignancy	2	3	3	3	3	2	3	2	3	2
most likely cancer	3	1	3	1	3	2	1	2	3	3
possibly cancer	3	3	1	3	1	1	3	1	1	1
probably cancer	3	2	2	2	2	2	2	1	2	2
most likely cancer of type A	3	b)	b)	b)	3	b)	1			
possibly cancer of type A	3	b)	b)	b)	1	b)	3			
probably cancer of type A	3	b)	b)	b)	2	b)	2			

continuing ranking direction[a)] texts from diagnoses	on formula II							
	↑	↑	↑	↑	↑	↑	↑	↑
malignancy cannot be excluded	5	4	3	2	2	3	2	2
strong suspicion of malignancy	6	5	5	5	3	4	5	6
malignancy cannot be entirely excluded	4	1	2	1	1	2	1	1
suspicion of malignancy	3	3	4	4	2	2	4	4
some suspicion of malignlity	1	2	1	3	1	1	3	3
most likely cancer	7	8	5	6	3	2	3	7
possibly cancer	2	6	2	4	1	1	1	5
probably cancer	6	7	4	5	2	2	2	7

---

a) ↑ means that "higher figure" (in formula I) has been inteterpreted so that 2 represents more than 1 and ↓ means that "higher figure" has been interpreted so that 1 represents more than 2.

b) Interpretation in words.

<u>Answers</u>

..................FROM 9 LINGUISTICIANS................
on formula I

<u>ranking direction</u>[a)] <u>texts from diagnoses</u>	↓	↓	↓	↑	↓	↑	↑ ↑[c)] ↓			↑
malignancy cannot be excluded	4	3	3	3	3	2	1	2[c)]	4	2
strong suspicion of malignancy	1	1	1	5	1	5	2	5	1	5
malignancy cannot be entirely excluded	5	2	5	1	4	1	1	1	5	1
suspicion of malignancy	2	3	2	4	2	4	2	4	2	4
some suspicion of malignancy	3	4	3	2	3	3	2	3	3	3
most likely cancer	2	1	1	2	1	3	2	3	1	2 3[d)]
possibly cancer	3	2	3	1	2	1	1	1	3	1
probably cancer	1	1	2	2	1	2	2	2	2	2 2
most likely cancer of type A	–	1	1	b)	b)	3	2	3	1	b)
possibly cancer of type A	–	2	3	b)	b)	1	1	1	3	b)
probably cancer of type A	–	1	2	b)	b)	2	2	2	2	b)

[a)] ↑ means that "higher figure" (in formula I) has been inteterpreted so that 2 represents more than 1 and ↓ means that "higher figure" has been interpreted so that 1 represents more than 2.
[b)] Interpretation in words.
[c)] As a patient in the left column; as a researcher in the right column
[d)] As a private person in the left column; as a researcher in the right column.

PAGE 131 FROM. SNOMED SYSTEMIZED NOMENCLATURE OF MEDICINE MICROGLOSSARY FOR SURGIAL PATHOLY SKOKIE, ILLINOIS 1980:

SNOMED System Information Qualifiers

General Information Qualifiers

Positive Qualifiers

HO = History of. . .

FH = Family history of. . .

PH = Past history of. . .

EO = Evidence of. . .

TR = Treatment required for. . .

Negative Qualifiers

NH = No history of. . .

NF = No family history of. . .

NP = No past history of. . .

NE = No evidence of. . .

NT = No treatment required for. . .

Qualifiers of Patient Problems

P1-P9 = Problem 1 to 9

CC = Chief complaint

Qualifiers for Types of Diagnosis

PX = Prior Diagnosis

AD = Admitting Diagnosis

PD = Preliminary Diagnosis

WD = Working Diagnosis

RD = Revised Diagnosis

PR = Principal Diagnosis

SE = Secondary Diagnosis

DX = Established Diagnosis

FD = Final Diagnosis (Discharge)

CD = Clinical Diagnosis

LD = Laboratory Diagnosis

CX = Cytology Diagnosis

AP = Pathology Diagnosis

XD = X-Ray Diagnosis

ND = Nursing Diagnosis

Qualifiers for Certainty of Diagnosis

Qualifiers for uncertain diagnoses should be used as infrequently as possible.

SD = Suspected Diagnosis (Question of/cannot exclude)

PB = Probable Diagnosis

PO = Possible Diagnosis

Special Information Qualifiers

DA = Diagnosis asymptomatic

HR = High risk of. . .

EX = Exposure to. . .

EX = Contact with. . .

SP = Status post

Qualifiers Used Mainly for Procedures

RE = Requested by patient

RP = Received procedure, therapy or drug

NO = Did not receive procedure, therapy or drug

AB = Procedure or test abnormal

Common Syntactic Linkage Symbols

NL = No link/end of statement

DT = due to

AW = associated with

FO = following

FB = followed by

AR = arising in

IN = in or of (T in T, or T of T, etc.)

CB = complicated by

PL = plus (in addition of. . .)

MI = minus (subtraction of. . .)

BY = for routes or vectors

TB = transmitted by (genetic)

CW = compatible with

CW = consistent with

IO = independent of

FW = for which was done

TW = treated with or by

RI = resulting in

DD = Death Diagnosis

DD = Major cause of death

APPENDIX C   in Swedish (English translation on pages C5–C8)

Gunhild Sandström   september 1984
Informationsbehandling-ADB
Lunds Universitet

BEGREPP INOM "bbb" SOM SKA DISKUTERAS MUNTLIGEN MED DIAGNOSTISÖRER

i grupper om 5 -6 personer

Begrepp:

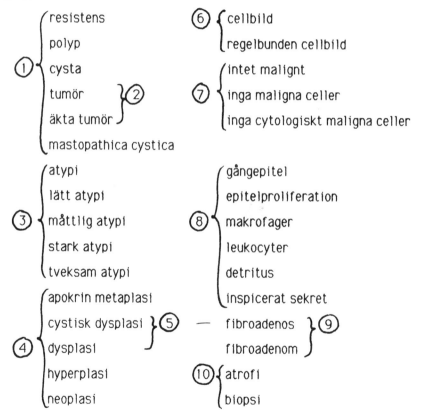

Ovanstående lista lämnades ut till dem som skulle diskutera, fastän utan
siffror och med diskussionsdatum utsatt.

Begreppen i listan har tagits fram efter genomläsning av ca 300 remisser om cancer eller misstänkt cancer och sedan fastställts som viktiga att studera i samråd med läkare vid "bbb".

FRÅGOR KRING BEGREPPEN:

(1)   Hur påverkas diagnosarbetet, om det i anamnesen finns medtaget något eller några av begreppen restistens, polyp, cysta, tumör, äkta tumör eller mastopathica cystica?

(2)   Hur skiljer du en tumör från en äkta tumör?

(3)   Vilka betingelser är nödvändiga för att säkerställa diagnosen
-atypi?
-lätt atypi?
-måttlig atypi?
-stark atypi?
-tveksam atypi?

(4)   Vilka funktioner fyller förstavelserna dys-, hyper-, meta- och neo-tillsammans med -plasi? Ändrar de betydelse om de föregås av ordet apokrin eller cystisk?

(5)   Vad är en diagnos? Vad är diagnoserna "dysplasi", "cystisk dysplasi" respektive "fibroadenos"?

(6)   Blir du oroad när cellbilden är regelbunden? Blir du oroad när cellbilden är oregelbunden? Vad menas med cellbild?

(7)   Vilka slutsatser tror du klinikern drar, om det i din diagnos står "Intet malignt", "Inga maligna celler" eller "Inga cytologiskt maligna celler"? Hur kan du skilja 'goda celler' från 'onda celler'?

(8)   Skriver du ut synpunkter om gångepitel, epitelproliferation, makrofager, leukocyter, detritus och inspicerat sekret i dina diagnoser? I så fall varför? Är klinikern intresserad? Har du blivit ålagd att göra det? Är det skick och bruk att göra så? Är det bra-att-ha-uppgifter för framtiden?

(9)   Finns någon skillnad mellan fibroadenos och fibroadenom?

(10) Vad innebär atrofi? Vad innebär biopsi?

LEXIKAL ÖVERSÄTTNING AV ANVÄNDA MEDICINSKA BEGREPP:

atrofi	förtvining
atypi	avvikande från det normala
biopsi	1: mikroskopisk undersökning av delar tagna från levande 2: undersökning om liv fanns
cysta	patologiska hålrum med särskild vägg och flytande eller grötigt innehåll
cytologi	cellära
detritus	till en kornig eller grötig massa sönderfallande degenerade celler eller vävnader
dysplasi	1: rubbning av den plastiska, formativa verksamheten 2: felaktig bildning, starkt avvikande från arttypen
epitel	det ytliga cellskikt som täcker hud och slemhinnor
fibroadenia	stark bindvävsökning i körtel eller körtelliknande organ
hyperplasi	vävnadsökning efter numerär cellnybildning
leukocyter	1: samlingsnamn för blodets samtliga vita celler (motsättning mot erytrocyter) 2: inskränkt polymorfkärniga vita celler (motsättning mot rundkärniga)
makrofager	monocyter (stora leukocyter) och alla fixa fagocyter (ätceller, dels makro- och dels mikrofager (små vita blodkroppar))
malignt	elakartat, om sjukdomar med elakartat förlopp
mastopathica cystica	form av kronisk mastit (inflammation i bröstkörteln), som anses disponibel för cancer
metaplasi	en vävnads omvandling utan mellanliggande modervävnad i en annan, vanligen efter en inledande återbildning till en mera indifferentierad embryonal form

neoplasi	nybildning av vävnader i bemärkelsen heteroplasi (nybildning av annan vävnad än den vävnad ur vilken den framväxer; synonym: alloplasi
polyp	berlockliknande utväxt från hud eller slemhinnor
proliferation	under tillväxt varande
resistens	palpabelt organ, sjuklig förändring
sekret	avsöndringsprodukt från körtlar
tumor	ansvällning, svulst, tumör, nybildning

Litteratur: Lindberg B I & Zetterberg B L (eds) "Medicinsk Terminologi" AB Nordiska Bokhandelns Förlag, Stockholm 1975

APPENDIX C   English translation.

Gunhild Sandström   September 1984
Information and Computer Sciences
Lund University, Sweden

CONCEPTS IN "bbb" THAT ARE TO BE DISCUSSED ORALLY WITH DIAGNOSTICIANS

in groups of 5-6 people

Concepts:

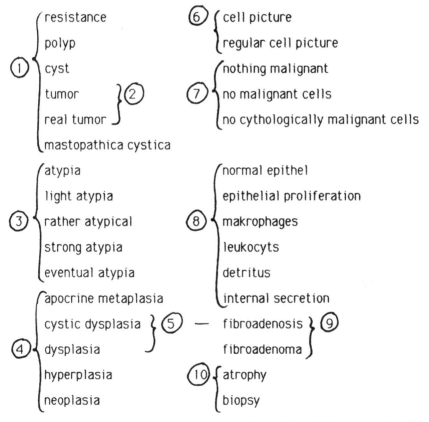

The above list was given to the participants but without figures and with
discussion date.

The concepts in the list have been chosen after my reading of 300 references about cancer or suspected cancer and then confirmed as important to study in corporation with a doctor at the "bbb".

QUESTIONS ABOUT THE CONCEPTS:

(1)   How is the diagnosis work being influenced, if there is any of the concepts 'restistance', 'polyp', 'tumor', 'real tumor' or 'mastopathica cystica' in the anamnesis?

(2)   How do you distinguish a tumor and a real tumor?

(3)   Which conditions are necessary to give the diagnosis
- atypia?   strong atypia
- light atypia?   hardly atypia
- rather atypical?

(4)   What functions are filled by the prefixes 'dys-', 'hyper-', 'meta-' and 'neo-' together with '-plasia'? Do they change their meaning if they are preceded by the word 'apocrine' or 'cystic'?

(5)   What is a diagnosis? What are the diagnoses "dysplasia", "cystic dysplasia" respectively "fibroadenosis"?

(6)   Do you become worried when the cell picture is regular? Do you become worried when the cell picture is irregular? What is the meaning of a cell picture?

(7)   Which conclusions do you think are drawn by a clinical doctor , if there is written "Nothing malignant", "No malignant cells" or "No cytholigal malignant cells"in your diagnosis? How do you distinguish between 'good cells' and 'bad cells'?

(8)   Do you write down your points of view about normal epithel, epithel proliferation, macrofags, leucocyts, detritus and internal secretion in your diagnoses? In these cases, why? Is the clinical doctor interested? Are you told to do so? Is it common or traditional to do so? Is it good-to-have-information for the future?

(9)   Is there any difference between fibroadenosis and fibroadenoma?

(10)   What is the meaning of 'atrophy'? What is the meaning of 'biopsi'?

LEXICAL TRANSLATION OF THE MEDICAL CONCEPTS USED:

atrophy — a diminution in the size of a cell, tissue or organ

atypia — the condition of being irregular or not conforming to type

biopsy — the removal and examination of tissue from a living body

cyst — any closed cavity or sac, that contains a liquid or semisolid material

cytology — the study of cells

detritus — particular matter produced by or remaining after the wearing away or disintegration of a substance or tissue

dysplasia — 1: alteration in size, shape, and organization of adult cells
2: abnormality of development

epithelium — the covering of internal and external surfaces of the body

fibroadenoma — a benign epithelial tumor containing fibrous tissue

fibroadenosis — a nodular condition of the breast not due to neoplasm

hyperplasia — the abnormal increase in the number of normal cells

leukocyts — 1: white blood cells
2: any colorless ameboid cell mass

makrophage — any of the larg, highly phagocytic cells with a small oval nucleus

malignant — tending to become progressively worse and to result in death

mastopathica cystica — a morbid condition of the mammary gland, with the formation of cysts

metaplasi — the change in the type of adult cells in a tissue to a form which is not normal for that tissue

neoplasia — the progressive multiplication of cells under conditions that would not elicit, or would cause cessation or multiplication of normal cells

polyp   a morbid excrescence from mucous membrane

proliferation   the reproduction of similar forms, especially of cells and
                   morbid cysts

resistance   palpable organ, morbid enlargement

secretion   the process of elaborating a specific product as a result of
                   the activity of a gland

tumor   morbid enlargement, a new growth of tissue in which the
                   multiplication of cells is uncontrolled and progressive

Reference: Dorland's (1974) Illustrated Medical Dictionary, 25th edition, W B
Saunders Co, Philadelphia, USA

APPENDIX D   in Swedish (English translation on pages D11-D20)

Gunhild Sandström   oktober 1984
Informationsbehandling-ADB
Lunds Universitet

UNDERSÖKNING AV ARBETE, SPRÅK OCH DATASYSTEM

VÄND EJ PÅ BLADET[a] FÖRRÄN DU ÖVERTYGAT DIG OM ATT DU FÖRSTÅR VAD
SOM STÅR PÅ DENNA SIDA!

Jag är forskare inom informationsbehandling-ADB och avlönas av Arbetarskyddsfonden, Styrelsen för Teknisk Utveckling och Lunds Universitet. Jag
har erhållit tillstånd att vid "XXX"-bolaget genomföra en undersökning på
några avdelningar rörande användning av datasystem och språk. Jag kommer
att ställa frågor till personer som arbetar direkt med eller beröres indirekt
av datasystem "aaa". På följande sidor kommer några diagram med utseendet

                              SKRIVBORD

fullt   *   *   *   *   *   *   * tomt
            ──

ordentligt   *   *   *   *   *   *   * stökigt
            ──

osv med 10-12 sådana här rader.

I dessa diagram ska du markera vad du associerar med SKRIVBORD. Om du
närmast tänker på SKRIVBORD som oerhört 'fullt' markera vid tecknet närmast "fullt" eller som alldeles 'tomt' markera vid tecknet närmast "tomt".
Nästan 'tomt' skulle kunna visas näst längst bort till höger. Exempel på mar-
kering ser du på raden "ordentligt......stökigt". Detta handlar om värdeomdömen
som du avger och du bestämmer själv vad som menas med "tomt" och "fullt"

─────────────────────
[a] Vända blad till D3 (i denna presentation)

163

och de fem mellanliggande ställena på raderna. Det är ca tio rader för varje BEGREPP och sammanlagt fem BEGREPP. På varje rad visar du var du vill associera mellan de båda ytterligheterna. Svara spontant - tänk inte för länge! Det gör inget om det ser motsägelsefullt ut. Ej heller bekymra dig för att du rätt vad det är upptäcker att samma saker kommer igen.

När du svarar ha ditt eget arbete i tankarna och det är datasystemet "aaa" som avses i förekommande fall.

Tack för din hjälp.

Innan du vänder blad[b] tala om vilken befattning, funktion eller titel du har på avdelningen:

....

I övrigt är denna undersökning anonym

(De närmast föjande tomma diagrammen visas komprimerade i denna bilaga. I undersökningen fanns ett diagram med tredubbelt radavstånd på varje sida)

---

[b] Vänder blad till D3 (i denna presentation)

DATASKÄRMSPRÅK

inexakt	*	*	*	*	*	*	*	exakt
rikt	*	*	*	*	*	*	*	fattigt
obegripligt	*	*	*	*	*	*	*	lättfattligt
roligt	*	*	*	*	*	*	*	tråkigt
korrekt	*	*	*	*	*	*	*	ogiltigt
fragmentariskt	*	*	*	*	*	*	*	fullständigt
schablonartat	*	*	*	*	*	*	*	nyansfullt
suddigt	*	*	*	*	*	*	*	klart
kantigt	*	*	*	*	*	*	*	följsamt
felaktigt	*	*	*	*	*	*	*	korrekt

DATORBASERAT BESLUTSUNDERLAG

banalt	*	*	*	*	*	*	*	intressant
aktuellt	*	*	*	*	*	*	*	inaktuellt
oanvändbart	*	*	*	*	*	*	*	användbart
korrekt	*	*	*	*	*	*	*	felaktigt
suddigt	*	*	*	*	*	*	*	klart
oviktigt	*	*	*	*	*	*	*	viktigt
naivt	*	*	*	*	*	*	*	sofistikerat
subjektivt	*	*	*	*	*	*	*	objektivt
tråkigt	*	*	*	*	*	*	*	engagerande
pålitligt	*	*	*	*	*	*	*	opålitligt
gammalt	*	*	*	*	*	*	*	färskt
tvingande	*	*	*	*	*	*	*	fritt

DATOR

billig	*	*	*	*	*	*	* dyr
lättskött	*	*	*	*	*	*	* svårskött
obekant	*	*	*	*	*	*	* välbekant
betydelsefull	*	*	*	*	*	*	* oväsentlig
tidsödande	*	*	*	*	*	*	* snabb
umbärlig	*	*	*	*	*	*	* oumbärlig
obegriplig	*	*	*	*	*	*	* begriplig
pålitlig	*	*	*	*	*	*	* lömsk
tröttande	*	*	*	*	*	*	* avlastande
intelligent	*	*	*	*	*	*	* dum
tidskrävande	*	*	*	*	*	*	* tidsödande

DITT YRKESKUNNANDE EFTER DATASYSTEMET BÖRJAT ANVÄNDAS VID DIN AVDELNING

förändrat	*	*	*	*	*	*	* oförändrat
kreativt	*	*	*	*	*	*	* förlamande
specialiserat	*	*	*	*	*	*	* breddat
övertaget	*	*	*	*	*	*	* berikat
passivt	*	*	*	*	*	*	* aktivt
stärkt	*	*	*	*	*	*	* uttunnat
avlastat	*	*	*	*	*	*	* tyngt
dåligt	*	*	*	*	*	*	* bra
engagerande	*	*	*	*	*	*	* monotoniserat
avtrubbat	*	*	*	*	*	*	* förlängt

DITT ARBETE EFTER DET ATT DATASYSTEM BÖRJAT ANVÄNDAS VID DIN
AVDELNING

enformigt	*	*	*	*	*	*	* rikt
tryggt	*	*	*	*	*	*	* osäkert
oviktigt	*	*	*	*	*	*	* betydelsefullt
bra	*	*	*	*	*	*	* dåligt
roligt	*	*	*	*	*	*	* tråkigt
fritt	*	*	*	*	*	*	* begränsat
tungt	*	*	*	*	*	*	* lätt
utan ansvar	*	*	*	*	*	*	* ansvarsfullt
informellt	*	*	*	*	*	*	* formellt
konserverande	*	*	*	*	*	*	* kreativt
viktigt	*	*	*	*	*	*	* likgiltigt

SAMMANFATTADE TYPVÄRDEN
från grupperna försäljare (SP)
orderbehandlare (OP)
speditörer (FA)
skeppningsassistenter (SA)
data experter (DE)

DATASKÄRMSPRÅK

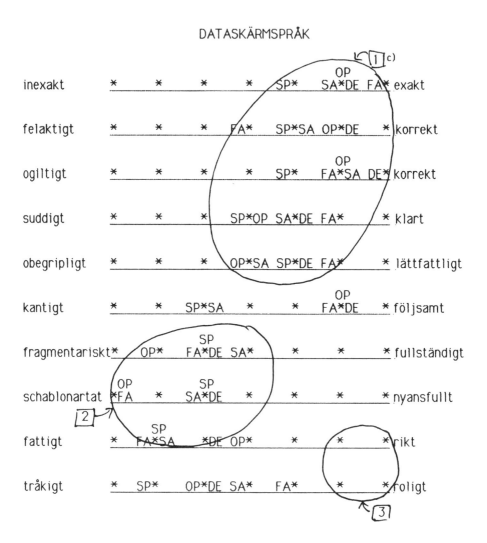

inexakt	*	*	*	* SP* OP SA*DE FA*	exakt
felaktigt	*	*	*	FA* SP*SA OP*DE *	korrekt
ogiltigt	*	*	*	* SP* OP FA*SA DE*	korrekt
suddigt	*	*	*	SP*OP SA*DE FA* *	klart
obegripligt	*	*	*	OP*SA SP*DE FA* *	lättfattligt
kantigt	*	*	SP*SA	* * OP FA*DE *	följsamt
fragmentariskt*	OP*	SP FA*DE SA*	*	* *	fullständigt
schablonartat	OP *FA	* SP SA*DE	*	* *	nyansfullt
fattigt	*	SP FA*SA *DE OP*	*	* *	rikt
tråkigt	* SP*	OP*DE SA*	FA*	* *	roligt

---

c) Dessa områden kommenteras i huvudtextens avsnitt 5.7.

DATORBASERAT BESLUTSUNDERLAG[d)]

$\boxed{4}$

| oanvändbart | * | * | * | * FA SP*SA DE*OP | * användbart |

| banalt | * | * | *FA | *SA | *OP SP*DE | * intressant |

| oviktigt | * | * | * | * OP *SP SA*FA DE* | viktigt |

| naivt | * | * | * | FA OP *SA SP*DE | * | * sofistikerat |

$\boxed{5}$

| inaktuellt | * | * | * | * DE *SA SP*FA OP* | aktuellt |

| felaktigt | * | *SA | * | *FA *SP OP*DE | * korrekt |

| suddigt | * | * | * | *SA SP*FA DE* OP* | klart |

$\boxed{6}$

| opålitligt | * | * | * | * SP*SA *DE OP* | pålitligt[e)] |

| gammalt | * | * | * | * SA* FA*OP DE* | färskt[f)] |

| objektivt | * OP*SA SP* | * | * | *DE | * subjektivt[e)] |

| tvingande | * | * FA*DE SP*OP | SA | * | * | *fritt |

| tråkigt | * | * SA* SP* OP*FA *DE | * engagerande |

$\boxed{7}$

[d)] Två ur gruppen SA har ej svarat alls.
[e)] I gruppen FA svarade lika många både-och.
[f)] I gruppen SP svarade lika många både-och.

DATOR

| oväsentlig | * | * | * | * | *FA SP*DE | * betydelsefull |

OP SA · 8

| umbärlig | * | * | * | * | SA*   SP*DE OP* | oumbärlig[g] |

| obekant | * | * | * | SP* | FA*SA OP*   DE* | välbekant |

| obegriplig | * | * | * | * | OP*SP SA*DE | * begriplig[g] |

OP

| lömsk | * | * | * | * | SA*FA SP*DE | * pålitlig |

FA

| svårskött | * | * | * | SP*DE SA*OP | * | * lättskött |

9

| tidsödande | * | * | * | * | SA*FA SP*DE OP* | snabb |

| tröttande | * | *SA | * | *FA SP*   DE*OP | * avlastande |

| dum | * | FA* | *SA | * | SP* | * | * intelligent[h] |

FA

| dyr | * | *SA OP*DE | * | SP* | * | * billig |

10

---

[g] I gruppen FA svarade lika många både-och.
[h] I grupperna OP och DE svarade lika många både-och.

DITT YRKESKUNNANDE EFTER DATASYSTEMET BÖRJAT ANVÄNDAS VID DIN
AVDELNING[i]

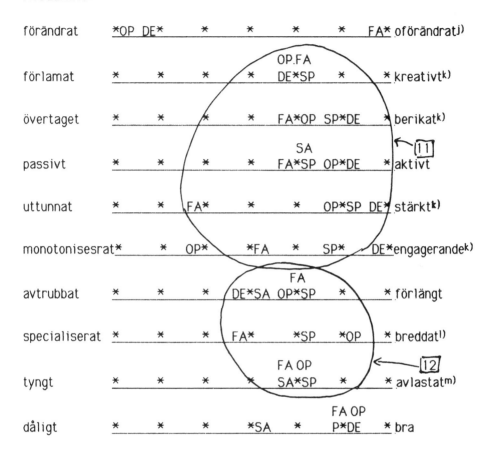

| förändrat | *OP DE* | * | * | * | * | FA* | oförändrat[j] |

förlamat   *   *   *   *   OP.FA DE*SP   *   * kreativt[k]

övertaget   *   *   *   *   FA*OP SP*DE   * berikat[k]

passivt   *   *   *   *   SA FA*SP OP*DE   * aktivt ←[11]

uttunnat   *   *   FA*   *   *   OP*SP DE* stärkt[k]

monotonisesrat *   *   OP*   *FA   *   SP*   DE*engagerande[k]

avtrubbat   *   *   *   FA DE*SA OP*SP   *   * förlängt

specialiserat   *   *   *   FA*   *SP   *OP   * breddat[l]

tyngt   *   *   *   *   FA OP SA*SP   *   * avlastat[m] ←[12]

dåligt   *   *   *   *SA   *   FA OP P*DE   * bra

---

[i] En person ur gruppen FA hade bara två markeringar.
[j] I grupperna SA och SP svarade lika många både-och.
[k]. I gruppen SA svarade lika många både-och.
[l] I grupperna SA och SP svarade lika många både-och.
[m] I gruppen DE svarade lika många både-och.

DITT ARBETE EFTER DET ATT DATASYSTEM BÖRJAT ANVÄNDAS VID DIN AVDELNING

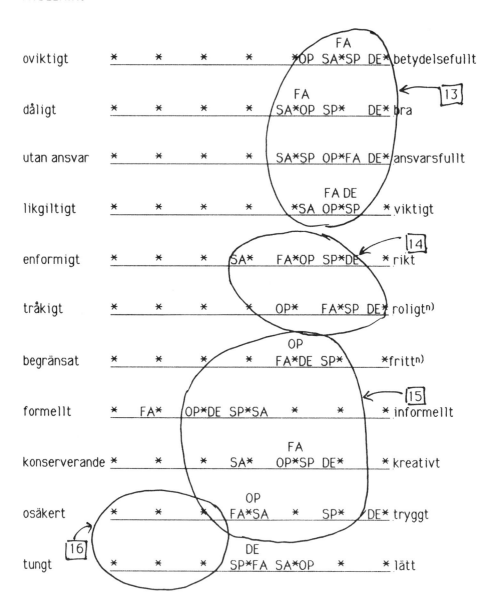

oviktigt	*	*	*	*	FA *OP SA*SP DE*	betydelsefullt
dåligt	*	*	*	*	FA SA*OP SP* DE*	bra
utan ansvar	*	*	*	*	SA*SP OP*FA DE*	ansvarsfullt
likgiltigt	*	*	*	*	FA DE *SA OP*SP	* viktigt
enformigt	*	*	*	SA*	FA*OP SP*DE	* rikt
tråkigt	*	*	*	*	OP* FA*SP DE*	roligt[n]
begränsat	*	*	*	*	OP FA*DE SP*	*fritt[n]
formellt	*	FA*	OP*DE SP*SA	*	*	* informellt
konserverande	*	*	*	SA*	FA OP*SP DE*	* kreativt
osäkert	*	*	*	OP FA*SA	* SP*	DE* tryggt
tungt	*	*	*	DE SP*FA SA*OP	*	* lätt

13
14
15
16

---

[n] I gruppen svarade lika många både-och.

Gunhild Sandström   October 1984
Information and Computer Sciences
Lund University

INVESTIGATION OF WORK, LANGUAGE AND COMPUTER SYSTEM

PLEASE, DO NOT TURN THE PAGE[a] UNTIL YOU ARE CONVINCED THAT YOU
UNDERSTAND WHAT IS ON THIS PAGE!

I am a researcher in information and computer sciences and am paid by The
Swedish Work Environment Fund and The National Swedish Board for Technical Development and Lund University. I have got permission to make an
investigation at some departments in "XXX" company concerning the use of
computer system and language. I am going too question some people who
work directly or indirectly with the system "aaa". On the following pages you
will see some diagrams looking like this:

WRITING TABLE

full   *   *   *   *   *   *   * empty

orderly   *   *   *   *   *   *   * messy

and so on with 10-12 such lines.

In these diagrams you shall mark what you associate with WRITING-TABLE
Ifö you primarily think of WRITING-TABLE as tremendously 'full' put a mark
at the sign nearest "full" or as completely 'empty' put a mark at the sign
nearest "empty". Almost 'empty' could be shown next furthest to the right. An
example of a mark is given at the line "orderly......messy". This is about values
that you give and you decide yourself the meaning of "empty" and "full" and

---

[a] Next page is D13 (in this presentation).

the five possible places between on the line. There are about ten lines for each CONCEPT and five in total concepts On each line you may show where you want to associate between the two extremes. Answer spontaneously – do not think too long! It does not matter if it looks constraining. Do not bother if you see the same things appear again.

When answering have your own work in mind and it is the computer system "aaa" which is referred to where approriate.

Thank you for your help.

Before you turn the page[b) write down your position, function or title at the department:

....

In other respects this investigation is anonymous.

(The following empty diagrams are shown compressed in this appendix. In the real investigation there was one diagram with triple line distances on each page)

---

b) Next page is D13 (in this presentation).

COMPUTER DISPLAY LANGUAGE

inexact	*	*	*	*	*	*	* exact
rich	*	*	*	*	*	*	* poor
incompre hensible	*	*	*	*	*	*	* intelligible
entertaining	*	*	*	*	*	*	* boring
correct	*	*	*	*	*	*	* invalid
fragmentary	*	*	*	*	*	*	* complete
stereotyped	*	*	*	*	*	*	* full of nuances
fuzzy	*	*	*	*	*	*	* clear
angular	*	*	*	*	*	*	* flexible
wrong	*	*	*	*	*	*	* correct

COMPUTERIZED DECISION BASES

trivial	*	*	*	*	*	*	* interesting
actual	*	*	*	*	*	*	* inactual
useless	*	*	*	*	*	*	* useable
correct	*	*	*	*	*	*	* wrong
fuzzy	*	*	*	*	*	*	* clear
unimportant	*	*	*	*	*	*	* important
naive	*	*	*	*	*	*	* sofisticated
subjective	*	*	*	*	*	*	* objective
boring	*	*	*	*	*	*	* engaging
reliable	*	*	*	*	*	*	* unreliable
old	*	*	*	*	*	*	* new
imperative	*	*	*	*	*	*	* unconstraining

COMPUTER

cheap	*	*	*	*	*	*	* expensive
easy to handle	*	*	*	*	*	*	* hard to handle
unknown	*	*	*	*	*	*	* wellknown
important	*	*	*	*	*	*	* unessential
time-consuming	*	*	*	*	*	*	* fast
dispensable	*	*	*	*	*	*	* indespensable
incomprehensible	*	*	*	*	*	*	* comprehensible
reliable	*	*	*	*	*	*	* crafty
tiring	*	*	*	*	*	*	* facilitating
intelligent	*	*	*	*	*	*	* foolish
time-demanding	*	*	*	*	*	*	* time-consuming

YOUR PROFESSIONAL KNOWLEDGE AFTER THE COMPUTER SYSTEM WAS
INTRODUCED INTO THE DEPARTMENT

altered	*	*	*	*	*	*	* unaltered
creative	*	*	*	*	*	*	* paralyzing
specialized	*	*	*	*	*	*	* broadened
overtaken	*	*	*	*	*	*	* enriched
passive	*	*	*	*	*	*	* active
strengthened	*	*	*	*	*	*	* weakened
facilitated	*	*	*	*	*	*	* burden
bad	*	*	*	*	*	*	* good
engaging	*	*	*	*	*	*	* monotonous
blunted	*	*	*	*	*	*	* extended

<u>YOUR WORK</u> AFTER THE COMPUTER SYSTEM WAS INTRODUCED INTO THE DEPARTMENT

dull	*	*	*	*	*	*	* rich
safe	*	*	*	*	*	*	* unsafe
unimportant	*	*	*	*	*	*	* significant
good	*	*	*	*	*	*	* bad
entertaining	*	*	*	*	*	*	* boring
free	*	*	*	*	*	*	* limiting
heavy	*	*	*	*	*	*	* easy
without responsibility	*	*	*	*	*	*	* responible
informal	*	*	*	*	*	*	* formal
conservative	*	*	*	*	*	*	* creative
important	*	*	*	*	*	*	* indifferent

SUMMARIZED TYPICAL VALUES
from the groups: sales personnel (SP)
order personnel (OP)
forwarding agents (FA)
shipping assistants (SA)
data experts (DE)

COMPUTER DISPLAY LANGUAGE

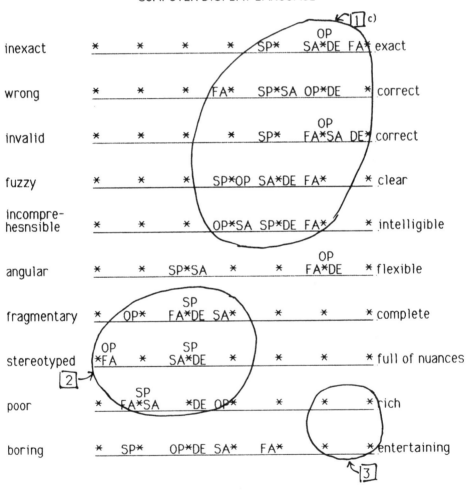

inexact	*	*	*	*	SP*	OP SA*DE FA*	exact
wrong	*	*	*	FA*	SP*SA OP*DE	*	correct
invalid	*	*	*	*	SP*	OP FA*SA DE*	correct
fuzzy	*	*	*	SP*OP SA*DE FA*		*	clear
incompre-hesnsible	*	*	*	OP*SA SP*DE FA*		*	intelligible
angular	*	*	SP*SA	*	*	OP FA*DE	* flexible
fragmentary	*	OP*	SP FA*DE SA*	*	*	*	complete
stereotyped	OP *FA	*	SP SA*DE	*	*	*	* full of nuances
poor	*	SP FA*SA	*DE OP*	*	*	*	rich
boring	*	SP*	OP*DE SA*	FA*	*	*	entertaining

[1] c)

[2]

[3]

---

c) These encircled fields are commented on in the main text.

COMPUTERIZED DECISION BASES[d]

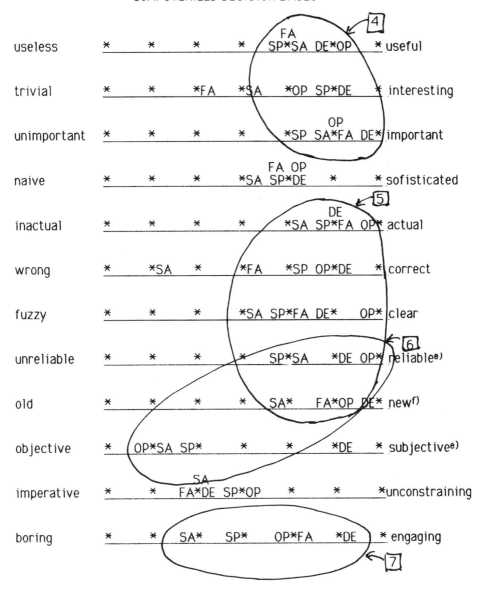

useless	*	*	*	*	FA SP*SA DE*OP	* useful	[4]
trivial	*	*	*FA	*SA	*OP SP*DE	* interesting
unimportant	*	*	*	*	OP *SP SA*FA DE*	important
naive	*	*	*	*SA	FA OP SP*DE	* * sofisticated
inactual	*	*	*	*	DE *SA SP*FA OP*	actual	[5]
wrong	*	*SA	*	*FA	*SP OP*DE	* correct
fuzzy	*	*	*	*SA	SP*FA DE* OP*	clear
unreliable	*	*	*	*	SP*SA *DE OP*	reliable[e]	[6]
old	*	*	*	*	SA* FA*OP DE*	new[f]
objective	*	OP*SA SP*	*	*	*DE	* subjective[e]
imperative	*	*	SA FA*DE SP*OP	*	*	*unconstraining
boring	*	*	SA*	SP*	OP*FA *DE	* engaging	[7]

---

d) Two people from the SA-group have not answered at all

e) In the FA-group the same amount of people answered both – and.

f) In the SP-group they answered both – and, to the same extent.

COMPUTER

unessential	*	*	*	*	OP SA *FA SP*DE	*	important
dispensable	*	*	*	*	SA* SP*DE OP*		indispensable[g]
unknown	*	*	*	SP*	FA*SA OP* DE*		wellknown
incomprehensible	*	*	*	*	OP*SP SA*DE	*	comprehensible[g]
crafty	*	*	*	*	OP SA*FA SP*DE	*	reliable
hard to handle	*	*	*	SP*DE SA*OP	FA	*	* easy to handle
timeconsuming	*	*	*	*	SA*FA SP*DE OP*		fast
tiring	*	*SA	*	*FA SP*	DE*OP	*	facilitating
foolish	*	FA*	*SA	*	SP*	*	* intelligent[h]
expensive	*	*SA OP*DE	FA	*	SP*	*	* cheap

Annotations: boxed 8, 9, 10.

---

[g] In the FA-group they answered both – and, to the same extent.
[h] In the groups OP and DE. they answered both and to the same extent.

YOUR PROFESSIONAL KNOWLEDGE AFTER THE COMPUTER SYSTEM WAS
INTRODUCED INTO THE DEPARTMENT[i]

altered	*OP DE*	*	*	*	*	FA*	unaltered[j]

paralyzing	*	*	*	*	OP.FA DE*SP	*	* creative[k]

overtaken	*	*	*	*	FA*OP SP*DE	* enriched[k]

passive	*	*	*	*	SA FA*SP OP*DE	* active	11

weakened	*	*	FA*	*	*	OP*SP DE* strengthened[k]

monotonous	*	*	OP*	*FA	*	SP*	DE*engaging[k]

blunted	*	*	*	FA DE*SA OP*SP	*	* extended

specialized	*	*	*	FA*	*SP	*OP	* broadened[l]

burden	*	*	*	*	FA OP SA*SP	*	* facilitated[m]	12

bad	*	*	*	*SA	*	FA OP P*DE	* good

---

[i] One person in the FA-group had just two marks.

[j] In the groups SA and SP they answered both – and, to the same extent.

[k] In the SA-group they answered both – and, to the same extent.

[l] In the groups SA and SP they answered both – and, to the same extent.

[m] In the DE-group they answered both – and, to the same extent.

YOUR WORK AFTER THE COMPUTER SYSTEM WAS INTRODUCED INTO THE
DEPARTMENT

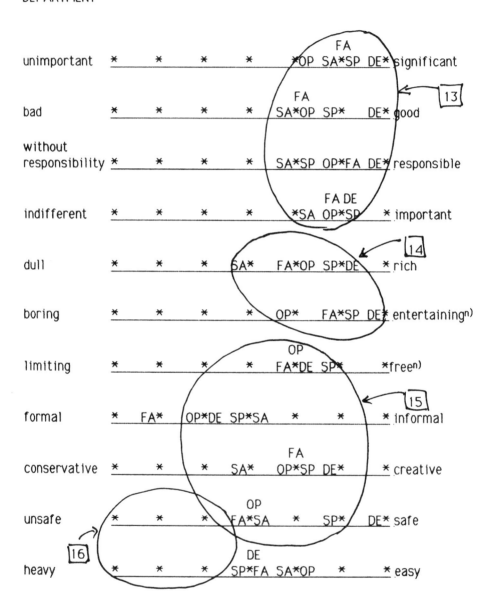

unimportant	*	*	*	*	FA *OP SA*SP DE* significant
bad	*	*	*	*	FA SA*OP SP* DE* good — 13
without responsibility	*	*	*	*	SA*SP OP*FA DE* responsible
indifferent	*	*	*	*	FA DE *SA OP*SP * important
dull	*	*	*	SA*	FA*OP SP*DE * rich — 14
boring	*	*	*	*	OP* FA*SP DE* entertaining[n]
limiting	*	*	*	*	OP FA*DE SP* *free[n]
formal	*	FA*	OP*DE SP*SA	*	* * informal — 15
conservative	*	*	*	SA*	FA OP*SP DE* * creative
unsafe	*	*	*	OP FA*SA	* SP* DE* safe
heavy	*	*	*	DE SP*FA SA*OP	* * easy — 16

---

[n] In the SA-group they answered both – and, to the same extent.

References

Alter S L (1980) "Decision Support Systems - Current Practice and Continuing Challenges" Addison Wesley, Philippines

Austin J L (1962) "How to do things with words" ed by Urmson J O & Sbisa M., Oxford University Press, Bristol 1980

Barr A & Feigenbaum E A (1981-82), eds "The Handbook of Artificial Intelligence" Volume I & II, William Kaufmann Inc/HeurisTech Press, California, USA

Barthes R (1964) "Billedets retorik" ur Fausing B & Larsen P "Visuel kommunikation" Medusa, Kobenhavn 1980 (The Original "Rhetorique de l´image" from the periodical Communications 4, 1964)

Bastick T (1982) "Intuition - how we Think and Act" John Wiley & Sons Bath, Avon U K

Bateson (1972) "Steps to an Ecology of Mind" Ballantine Books, New York

Beer S (1966) "Decision and Control - the Meaning of Operational Research and Management Cybernetics" John Wiley & Sons, London

Berger P L & Luckmann (1966) "The Social Construction of Reality - A Treatise in the Sociology of Knowledge" Anchor Books, Doubleday Co, Garden City, N Y 1967

Berglind J (1984) "Om standard i allmänhet" ur "Att formalisera Informationssystem" red H-E Nissen, Lunds Universitet, Informationsbehandling-ADB, Lund

Bergmann G (1964) "Logic and Reality" , The University of Wisconsin Press, Madison

Björn-Andersen N (1976) "Organizational Aspects of Systems Design" DATA No 12, R&D pp 75-80

Boar B H (1984) "Application Prototyping" John Wiley & Sons, USA

Boden M A (1981) "Minds and Mechanisms - Philosophical Psychology and Computational Models" the Harvester Press Ltd, Brighton, Great Britain

Boland R J Jr (1978) "The Process and Product of System Design" from Management Science, Vol 24, No 9, May 1978, pp 887-898

Bubenko J Jr (1979) "Data Models and their Semantics", the INFOTECH State-of-the-Art Conference on "Data Design", Sept 1979 London

Bubenko J Jr, ed (1983) "Information Modeling" Chartwell-Bratt Ltd, Lund Sweden

Bubenko J Jr & Lindencrona E (1984) "Konceptuell modellering - informationsanalys" Studentlitteratur, Lund Sweden

Bunge M (1967) "Scientific Research I - The Search for System" Springer Verlag, Berlin

Checkland P (1981) "Systems Thinking, Systems Practice" John Wiley & Sons Ltd, Chichester, U K

Chen P P S (1976) "The Entity-Relationship Model - Toward a Unified View of Data" ACM Transactions on Database Systems, vol 1 no 1, March 1976, pp 9-36, New York NY

Cherry C (1957) "On Human Communication" the MIT Press, Massachusetts, USA, 1971

Churchman C W (1971) "The Design of an Inquiring System: basic concepts of systems and organizations" Basic Books

Clocksin W F & Mellish C S (1981) "Programming in Prolog" Springer--Verlag, New York

Codd E F (1970) "A Relationaal Model of Data for Large Shared Data Banks" in Communications of the ACM, vol 13 no 6, June 1970 pp 377-387, New York NY

Codd E F (1979) "Extending the Database Relational Model to Capture More Meaning" in Transactions on Database Systems, vol 4 no 4, Dec 1979, pp 397-434, New York NY

Cohen P R & Feigenbaum E A (1982) eds "The Handbook of Aritficial Intelligence" Volume III, William Kaufmann Inc/Pitman, London

Danielsson A (1975) "Företagsekonomi - en översikt" Studentlitteratur, Lund Sweden

Date C J (1980) "An Introduction to the Unified Database Language (UDL)" in Conferences on Very Large Data Bases 6, ed by Lochovsky & Taylor, pp 15-29

Davis R (1976) "Applications of Meta Level Knowledge to the Construction Maitenance and Use of Large Knowledge Bases" Report No STAN-CS-76-564, Computer Sciences Department, Stanford University (Doctoral dissertation)

De Maio A (1980) "Socio-technical Methods for Information Systems Design" in "The Information Systems Environment", Proceedings from the IFIP TC8.2 Working Conference, ed by Lucas H C, Land F F, Lincoln T J and Supper K, Bonn, West Germany, June 1979

De Monthoux P G (1981) "Doktor Kant och den oekonomiska rationaliseringen - Om det normativas betydelse för företagens, industrins och teknologins ekonomi" Korpen, Göteborg, Sweden

Dennett D C (1983) "Intentional Systems in Cognitive Ethology: The "Panglossian Paradigm defended" from "The Behavioral and Brain Sciences" (1983) 6, pp 343-355, Cambridge University Press, USA

Dorland´s (1974) Illustrated Medical Dictionary, 25th edition, W B
    Saunders Co, Philadelphia USA

Doyle J (1980) "A Model for Deliberation, Action and Introspection"
    Tech Report AI-TR-581, AI Laboratory, Massachusetts Institute
    of Technology USA (Doctoral dissertation)

Eco U (1971) "Den frånvarande strukturen" Bo Cavefors Bokförlag AB, Lund
    Sweden (Original title "La struttura assente" Casa Ed. Valentino
    Bompiani & Co, Italy 1969)

Ekenberg B (1985), Information and Computer Science, Lund University,
    Lund, Sweden, personal communication

Flensburg P (1984) "Lägesrapport från ett Aktionsorienterat Forsknings-
    projekt" Informationsbehandling-ADB, Lunds Universitet, Lund
    Sweden

Floyd C (1983) "A Systematic Look at Prototyping", Working Conference on
    Prototyping, Belgium

Friis S (1984) "Prototyping - an Evolutionary Systems Development"
    in report of the Seventh Seminar on Systemeering part I, ed by
    M Sääksjärvi, Helsinki School of Economics, Helsinki

Galtung J (1977) "Methodology and Ideology" volume one, Christian El-
    jers, Copenhagen

Gingras L & McLean E R (1982) " Designers and Users of Information
    Systems: A Study in Differing Profiles" in Proceedings of the
    3rd International Conference on Information Systems ed by
    Ginzberg & Ross, Ann Arbor Michigan

Glimell H (1975) "Designing Interactive Systems for Organizational Change"
    BAS ek för, Göteborg Sweden

Goldkuhl G (1980) "Information Systems Specification - Establishing a
    Formal Language Intersubjectivity among Users" in Lyytinen K &
    Peltola E (eds) Jyväskylä, Finland

Goldkuhl G & Lyytinen K (1982) "A Language Action View of Information
    System" in Ginzberg M & Ross C A (eds) "Proceedinggs of the
    Third International Conference on Information Systems" Ann
    Arbor, Michigan

Goldschlager L & Lister A (1982) "Computer Science - A Modern Introduc-
    tion" Prentice-Hall, London

Gorry A & Scott Morton M (1971) "A Framework for Management Information
    Systems" Sloan Management Review, Volume 13, No 1, pp 55 - 70

van Griethuysen J J,ed (1982) "Concepts and Terminology for the Con-
    ceptual Schema and the Information Base" ISO/TC97/ SC5 - N 695
    International Federation of Information Processing

Grönmo S (1982) "Forholdet mellom kvalitative og kvantitative metoder i
    samfunnsforskningen" ur "Kvalitative metoder i samfunnsforskning"
    red av Holter H & Kalleberg R, Universitetsforlaget, Drammen
    Norway

Göranzon B (1978) red "Ideologi och systemutveckling" Studentlitteratur
    Lund Sweden

Göranzon B och Josefson I (1980) "Fantasi och verklighet vid datorise-
    ring - om yrkeskunskapens fragmentering" ur "Fragmentering av
    kunskap" rapport från ett seminarium 1979, red A-M Thunberg,
    Delegationen för långsiktmotiverad forskning, Stockholm

Haack S (1978) "Philosophy of Logics" Cambridge University Press,
    Cambridge, Great Britain

Habermas J (1979) "Communications and the Evolution of Society" Heine-
    mann, London

Hayek F (1937) "Economics and Knowledge" in "Economica" February

Hedberg B (1974) "Computer Systems to Support Industrial Democracy" in
    Mumford E & Sackman H (eds) "Human Choice and Computers" North-
    -Holland, Amsterdam

Hedberg B & Mumford E (1979) "Some Theoretical Ideas of Relevance to
    Systems Design" in Björn-Andersen N, Hedberg B, Mercer D,
    Mumford E, Sole⁻ A (eds) "The Impact of Systems Change in Orga-
    nizations" Sijthoff & Noordhoff, Netherlands

Hyyninen R, Wadman B, Åberg H (1984) "Att skriva patientjournaler -
    sjukhistoria och klinisk undersökning - lagen - språket"
    Studentlitteratur, Lund Sweden

Höyer R (1979) "System Development as a Learning Process in a Firm; Some
    Pedagogical Requirements for System Development Models" in
    "Report of the Scandinavian Research Seminar on Systemeering
    Models" ed by Järvi T & Nurminen M, Helsinki

Israel J (1979) "The Language of Dialectics and the Dialectics of
    Language" Harvester Press, Great Britain

Israel J (1982) "Om konsten att blåsa upp en ballong inifrån" Korpen,
    Göteborg Sweden

Israel J (1985) Department öf Sociology, Lund University, Lund, perso-
    nal communication in Februar 1985

Ivanov K (1972) "Quality-Control of Information - on the Concept of
    Accuracy of Information in Data-Banks and in Management
    Information Systems" Dissertation, Faculty of the Royal
    Institute of Technology, Stockholm Sweden

Ivanov K (1984) "Systemutveckling och ADB-ämnets utveckling" ur
    "Systemutveckling - av Vem, för Vem och Hur?" red av H-E Nissen,
    Arbetarskyddsfonden, Stockholm Sweden

Jenkins M A (1983) "Prototyping: A Methodology for the Design and Development of Application Systems" discussing paper no 227, Indiana University

Järvinen P (1983) "Observations of a Programming Process: The ABC case" in "The ABC System - a Collection of Research Articles" Department of Mathematical Sciences, University of Tampere, Finland

Järvinen P (1984) "On Selection of Methods for Studying Interactive Systems - Analysis of the Topic as Structured by the Keystroke-level Model" in Report of the Seventh Scandinavian Research Seminar on Systemeering, Part I, ed by M Sääksjärvi, Helsinki School of Economics, Helsinki

Keen P G W (1980) "Adaptive Design for Decision Support Systems" Data-Base Vol 12 Nos 1-2 p 15-25

Kent W (1978) "Data and reality", North-Holland, Amsterdam, 1984

Kerlinger F N (1964) "Foundations of Behavioral Research", Holt, Rinehart and Winston, N Y (1973)

"Kompendium i medicinsk informationsbehandling" (1980), Universitetet i Linköping, Sweden

Kubicek H (1984) "Benutzerbeteiligung und Mitbestimmung bei der Planung von Anwendungen der Informationstechnik - Unterschiedliche Einschätzungen aus Arbeitgeber- und Arbeitnehmersicht und Argumente fur einen Kompromiss" from "Planung in der Datenverarbeiten" at Wissenschaftszentrum Bonn-Bad-Godesberg

Langefors B (1963) "Some Approaches to the Theory of Information Systems" Nordisk Tidskrift för Informationsbehandling (BIT) vol 3, pp 229-254, Copenhagen

Langefors B (1966) "Theoretical Analysis of Information Systems", Studentlitteratur, Lund, Sweden 1973

Langefors B (1970) "A Concept of "Concepts" - Memory Economy" IB-ADB 70 No 29, Informationsbehandling-ADB, Kungl Tekn Högskolan, Stockholm

Langefors B & Sundgren B (1975) "Information Systems Architecture" Mason/Charter Publishers, New York

Lanzara G F & Mathiassen L (1984) "Mapping Situations within a System Development Project - An Intervention Perspective on Organizational Change" University of Aarhus, Denmark

Lindberg B I & Zetterberg B L (eds) "Medicinsk Terminologi", AB Nordiska Bokhandelns Förlag, Stockholm

Lindholm S (1979) "Vetenskap, verklighet och paradigm" AWE/Gebers, Stockholm

Lindholm S (1980) "Kunskapens fragmentering - tankar i början av ett projekt" ur "Fragmentering av kunskap" rapport från ett seminarium 1979, red A-M Thunberg, Delegationen för långsiktmotiverad forskning, Stockholm

Lindholm S (1982) "Från visdom till kunskap på burk" TANKESTRECK, UMIL, Pedagogiska Institutionen, Stockholms Universitet

Lindholm S (1983) "Intuition, kunskapsfragmentering och helhetssyn" TANKESTRECK, UMIL, Pedagogiska Institutionen, Stockholms Universitet

Lyytinen K (1981) "Language Oriented Development of Information Systems - Methodological and Theoretical Foundations" Licentiate Thesis, University of Jyväskylä, Finland

Lyytinen K & Lehtinen E (1984) "Discourse Analysis as an Information System Specification Method" in report of the Seventh Seminar on Systemeering, part I, ed by M Sääksjärvi, Helsinki School of Economics, Helsinki

McGregor (1960) "The Human Side of Enterprise" McGraw-Hill Book Co, New York

Mitroff I (1980) "Towards a Logican Methodology for ´Real-World´ Problems" in Bjorn-Andersen N (ed): "The Human Side of Information Processing" North-Holland, Amsterdam, Proceedings of the Copenhagen Conference on Computer Impact-78, October 1978

Morris C (1964) "Signification and Significance", MIT Press, Cambridge, Massachusetts, USA

Nilsson K (1984) "Några problemställningar kring datamodelleringg och interaktiva databastillämpningar" Umeå Universitet, Institutionen för informationsbehandling, Administrativ databehandling, Umeå, Sweden

Nissen H-E (1976) "On Interpreting Services Rendered by Specific Computer Applications" Dissertation, Department of Information Processing, Royal Institute of Technology, Stockholm

Nissen H-E (1981) "When People Design an Information System - then the System Designs People" Department of Administrative Data Processing, University of Lund, Proceedings of the IFIP TC 8 Working Conference on Evolutionary Systems, Budapest 1-3 September 1981, edited by John Hawgood, North-Holland Publ Co, Amsterdam 1982

Nissen H-E (1983) "Att formalisera informationssystem - möjligheter, problem, innebörder och avsikter" C/D-Kurs PM 2, Umeå Universitet, Umeå, Sweden

Nissen H-E (1984a) "Towards a Two-faced Theory of Information Systems" Department of Information an Computer Science, Lund University, Sweden

Nissen H-E (1984b) personal communication in November 1984

Nissen H-E (1985) "Mot sammanhängande teorier för alla om informations-system" institutionen för informationsbehandling-ADB, Lunds Universitet, Lund, Sweden

Nissen H-E & Andersen E (1977) "Systemering - Verksamhetsbeskrivning" Studentlitteratur, Lund, Sweden

Nissen H-E, Carlsson S, Nadel D (1981) "Why is User Orientation a Must in Information Systems Development" Department of Information and Computer Sciences, University of Lund

Nissen H-E, Carlsson S, Flensburg P, Holmberg K-Å, Sandström G & Wormell I (1982) "User Oriented Information Systems - A research program" Department of Information and Computer Sciences, University of Lund, Lund Sweden

Nissen H-E, Carlsson S, Flensburg P, Friis S, Sandström S (1983) "Forskningsprogram till ASF: Användarnära besluts- och informationssystem - deras bruk och utveckling" Informationsbehandling--ADB, Lunds Universitet

Nissen H-E & Holmberg K-Å (1982) "Theoretical Frames of Reference for Research on User Oriented Information Systems" Department of Information and Computer Sciences, Lund University, Sweden, June 1982

Nurminen M I (1980) "On Teleological Aspects of Information and Information Systems" in Lyytinen K & Peltola (eds) "Report of the Third Scandinavian Research Seminar on Systemeering Models" Institute of Computer Science, University of Jyväskylä, Finland

Nurminen M I (1982) "Human-Scale Information System" Institutt for Informasjonsvitenskap, Universitetet i Bergen, Norge

Ogden C K & Rickards I A (1923) "The meaning of Meaning - A Study of the Influence of Language upon Thought and of the Science of Symbolism" Routledge & Kegan Paul Ltd, London 1969

Osgood C et al (1957) "The Measurement of Meaning", University of Illinois Press, Urbana, Chicago and London 1967

Peirce C S (1931-35) "Collected Papers" Harvard University Press, Cambridge

Polanyi M (1966) "The Tacit Dimension", Anchor Books, Garden City, N Y

Postman N & Weingartner C (1971) "Teaching as a Subversive Activity" Penquin Education Specials

Radnitzky G (1970) "Contemporary Schools of Metascience" Läromedelsförlagen, Lund Sweden

Rapoport R N (1971) "Three dilemmas in Action Research" in "Human Relations" Vol 23 No 6

Rommetveit R (1974) "On Message Structure" John Wiley & Sons, London 1977

Rubin M L (1972) "Introduction to the Systems Life Cycle", Brandon System Press, London

Ryle G (1949) "The Concept of Mind" Penguin Books Ltd, Harmondsworth, Great Britain 1963

Sandström G (1981) "Improved Retrieval from Information Systems (IRIS) - Some Foundations for Research" Information and Computer Sciences, University of Lund, Sweden

Sandström G (1982) "Improved Retrieval from Information Systems" (IRIS) project draft, Information and Computer Sciences, University of Lund

Sandström G (1984a) "Innebörder hos fenomen som uttryckes i databaser" ur symposierapport från "Systemutveckling - av Vem, för Vem och Hur?" red av H E Nissen vid Lunds Universitet, Arbetarskyddsfonden Stockholm

Sandström G (1984b) "How to Understand and Act on Phenomena Expressed in Data Bases - Research Problems and Frames of References" in report of the Seventh Scandinavian Research Seminar on Systemeering, ed by M Sääksjärvi, Helsinki School of Economics, Helsinki

Sandström G (1984c) "Different Meanings of Concepts and Propositions in an Information System" Information and Computer Sciences, Lund University, Lund, Sweden

Sandström G (1984d) "An Intervening Method to Facilitate Systems Development ´in the Small´" Information and Computer Sciences, Lund University, Lund, Sweden

Sandström G & Wormell I (1980) "Studier av modeller för systemutveckling hos Lantbrukskooperationen" Lunds Universitet, Informationsbehandling-ADB, Lund

Searle J R (1969) "Speech Acts - An Essay in the Philosophy of Language" Cambridge University Press, New York

Senko M E, Altman E B, Astrahan M M & Fehder P L (1973) "Data Structures and Accessing in Data Base Systems" IBM Systems Journal, vol 12, no 1, pp 30-93

Senko M E (1977) "Data Structures and Data Accessing in Data Base Systems Past, Present and Future" IBM Systems Journal vol 16, no 3 1977, pp 208-257

Sibley E H, ed (1976) "Special Issue on Data Base Management Systems" ACM Computing Surveys, vol 8, no 1, March 1976

Siu R G H (1957) "The Tao of Science" M I T Press, Cambridge, Masachusetts

SNOMED (1980) "Systemized Nomenclature of Medicine - Microglossary for Surgial Pathology, Skokie, Illinois

Sol H G (1983) "Prototyping: A Methodological Assessment" Cris II Conference, York, England

Sorokin P A (1941) "Social and Cultural Dynamics" Volym IV, American Book Company, New York

Sowa J F (1984) "Conceptual Structures - Information Processing in Mind and Machine" Addison-Wesley, Reading, Massachusetts

Stamper R (1973) "Information in Business and Administrative Systems", B T Batsford Ltd, London

Sundgren B (1973) "An Infological Approach to Data Bases" University of Stockholm, Department of Information Processing, Stockholm, Sweden

Sundgren B (1975) "Theory of Data Bases" Petrocell-Mason-Charter, New York

Susman G I & Evered R D (1978) "An assessment of the Scientific Merits of Action Research", Administrative Science Quarterly, December 1978, pp 582-603

Sussman G J (1973) "A Computational Model of Skill Acquisition" AI Tech Report 297, AI Laboratory, Massaachusetts Institute of Technology (Doctoral dissertation)

Teorey T J & Fry J P (1982) "Design of Database Structures" Prentice Hall, Englewood Cliffs N J

Toulmin S E (1958) "The Uses of Argument" University Press, Cambridge

Tschudi F (1984) "Om nödvändigheten av syntese mellom kvantitative og kvalitative metoder" ur "Kvalitative metoder i samfunnsforskning" red Holter H & Kalleberg R, Universitetsforlaget, Oslo

Ullman J D (1982) "Principles of Data Systems" 2 ed, Computer Science Press

Wallin E (1980) "Vardagslivets generativa grammatik" PhD thesis, Liber, Lund Sweden

Watzlawick P, Helmick Beavin J, Jackson D D (1967) "Pragmatics of Human Communication - a Study of Interactional Patterns, Pathologies and Paradoxes" W W Norton & Company Inc, New York

Watzlawick P, Weakland J H, Fisch R (1974) "CHANGE - Principles of Problem Formation and Problem Resolution" W W Norton & Company Inc, New York

Watzlawick P (1978) "The Language of Change - Elements of Therapeutic Communication" Basic Books, New York

Wedberg A (1945) "Den nya logiken" andra delen, Verdandis Småskrifter
    N:r 478, Albert Bonniers Förlag, Stockholm

Wilson B (1984) "Systems: Concepts, Methodologies, and Applications"
    John Wiley & Sons Ltd, Chichester, U K

Winograd T (1972) "Understanding Natural Language" Academic Press, New
    York

Winograd T (1973) "A Procedural Model of Language Understanding" in Schank
    R C & Colby K M "Computer Models of Thoughts and Language", W H
    Freeman, San Francisco

Wunderlich D (1979) "Foundation of Linguistics" Cambridge